# ONE SELF

## LIFE AS A MEANS
## OF TRANSFORMATION

## PHILIP JACOBS

First published by O Books, 2006
An imprint of John Hunt Publishing Ltd., The Bothy, Deershot Lodge, Park
Lane, Ropley, Hants, SO24 0BE, UK
office@johnhunt-publishing.com
www.o-books.net

USA and Canada
NBN
custserv@nbnbooks.com
Tel: 1 800 462 6420 Fax: 1 800 338 4550

Australia
Brumby Books
sales@brumbybooks.com
Tel: 61 3 9761 5535 Fax: 61 3 9761 7095

Singapore
STP
davidbuckland@tlp.com.sg
Tel: 65 6276 Fax: 65 6276 7119

South Africa
Alternative Books
altbook@global.co.za
Tel: 27 011 792 7730 Fax: 27 011 972 7787

Design: Stuart Davies
Cover design: Book Design, London

ISBN-13: 978 1 905047 67 3
ISBN-10: 1 905047 67 3

Printed by Maple-Vail, USA

# ONE SELF

## LIFE AS A MEANS
## OF TRANSFORMATION

PHILIP JACOBS

BOOKS

Winchester, UK
Washington, USA

# ONE SELF
## LIFE AS A MEANS OF TRANSFORMATION

*One Self expresses the truth at the heart of the world's mystical and philosophical traditions in a simple, direct and practical way.*

*We can start to find meaning in our lives when we see all the varied things that happen to us, including illness and bereavement, as part of the process of letting go of lesser levels of identity. We can then find our true Being that is ever present and beyond change and suffering. We learn to trust the process of life's unfolding, as we are led on a journey to discover a great treasure that we all possess, yet are unaware of. In doing this we also prepare ourselves for that ultimate moment of letting go, the death of the physical body.*

*So many books of personal philosophy and psychology today get bogged down in bias and belief. This is a rare exception. Philip Jacobs cuts to the heart of the philosophy of non duality, writing from personal experience, and leads us down a simple path that all can follow. The more people that buy this book the better the world will be because everyone will be happy with their own circumstances.*

**MARTIN REDFERN,**
*SENIOR PRODUCER, BBC RADIO SCIENCE UNIT*

*Philip Jacobs shows a profound understanding of the unity of life and the interconnectedness of everything within the world. He shows how events which may appear to be random can also be seen as part of our life's path when looked at on a wider time* scale. *He gives clear guidance on how to surrender to illness and see it as a positive event through which the individual can grow. He shows the importance of remaining in the now, where the action happens and where comfort and solace can be obtained. He has a fund of the most wonderful stories to illustrate his points. He discusses the true meaning of freedom and takes the view that we are all part of a single unity and that everything about our lives is taken care of when looked at from this broader perspective. This is a compelling and life enhancing book for anyone having to face a long term illness, but also so wise that it can help any of us to understand our path in life even if we are not so severely challenged.*

**PETER FENWICK,**
SCIENTIFIC AND MEDICAL NETWORK

*In a concentrated piece of writing, Philip Jacobs propels us into a wider plain of existence. He invites us to abandon our petty worries and experience a deeply positive world full of love and possibilities.*

**KAFFE FASSETT**

FOR D.H.J AND F.C.R
WITH LOVE.

# CONTENTS

# INTRODUCTION

The purpose of this book is to give confidence to people, particularly those having a difficult time due to adverse life circumstances. It is to show that at every moment we are being lovingly led and looked after and that ultimately all our varied life experiences are about the discovery of our true Selves; who we really are at the depths of our beings and how, in discovering that and in living our lives to the full, we prepare ourselves for that ultimate moment of letting go, the death of the physical body.

This book is not intended to give answers to any of life's mysteries but rather, by using the non-dual model, to paint a picture of some of the ways we can look at our lives from a different point of view in the hope that some of this may connect with each individual's experience and hence be a stepping stone towards each person formulating their own model of reality and integrating their lives into a larger whole.

# ACKNOWLEDGMENTS

I would like to offer profound thanks to Dr Francis Roles (1901-1982). Without his influence and the seeds he sowed this book would not have been possible. I would also like to thank Anne Garten, Solveig McIntosh and Karen Sanderson for proofreading and help with preparation of the text.

# CHAPTER 1

# ONE CONSCIOUSNESS

In our journey through life we will encounter a great variety of different events and experiences, some of which we can understand and others that seem to serve no useful purpose. Eventually we may be drawn to question the nature of life and reality. We may ask such questions as, "Does life have a purpose or is it all just a matter of chance and the survival of the fittest?" "Are we just physical entities that are coming from nowhere, going nowhere and exist only as the result of physical evolution?"

There are many different models of reality, or ways of looking at ourselves and the world about us. Yet all our formulations and explanations of reality are metaphors, since

I suspect that reality is inexplicable to mere mortals such as ourselves. Yet our basic model or view of reality is very important, since it is from this that all of our actions and reactions stem. So we need metaphors or approximations of the truth, and at different times in our lives different metaphors appeal to us, according to our needs.

A model of reality can be a useful aid to thought. It acts as a metaphor or approximation to something that is beyond expression. It is rather like a symbol; much knowledge and experience is contained in a 'nutshell'. It can act as a mental framework with which to understand the world and all experience, though as with all traditions and ideas, it should be a springboard for thought and not a limitation as it connects with the individual's own unique experience. As the Buddha said:

It is not what you believe that is important, but what you do and what you are and what you feel. Only if a teaching is consistent with your own experience should you accept it.

We are all unique and capable of understanding and expressing reality in a unique way, for the creation is one of infinite variety. And if the Buddha can say that about his own teaching how much more does it apply to what is written in this book?

The model that I have found most helpful in understanding the world and myself is known as Non-dualism. Non-duality is not exclusive to any one tradition; rather it lies at the heart of all the world's great religious and mystical traditions. But it has one pitfall; it cannot be rationally explained but only experienced at first hand and then hinted at by metaphors and symbols. Thus it can appear paradoxical, not because it is, but because this is how reality can appear from a purely rational level.

Non-dualism literally means 'Not two'. In this model, as I understand it, the whole universe and everything contained in it is an expression of one undivided whole or Universal Consciousness that contains not the slightest element of opposite. Hence what appear to be opposites are just the variable aspects of this one undivided whole. From this perspective the universe is perceived as the perfect manifestation of spirit right down to the smallest detail. There is nothing that is outside this Consciousness, from which it is thus impossible to deviate.

All of us are aspects of this Consciousness. It is as if there is just one Being looking out through all of our different eyes, yet we mistakenly see ourselves as separate from each other and separate from the world around.

The implications of this model are very far reaching, regarding the way in which we live our lives and view reality. For it implies that whatever we experience in our lives is a part or aspect of that One Consciousness. This includes both the things we understand and the things we do not understand or as Sir Laurens van der Post once suggested, we have to learn to trust our bad luck as much as our good luck, as it's all a part of the same thing.

It was Albert Einstein who once said that the most

important question we can ask ourselves is whether the universe is a friendly place. It is this fundamental belief that determines how we respond to life. If we see the world as chaotic and full of chance, then it is a frightening place, where anything could happen at any moment if we put a foot wrong, or even if we don't someone else will. This can lead to belief in the survival of the fittest, and a need to control the world about us, and a need to manipulate or dominate others, for surely without our intervention events will not go the way we think they should. From this viewpoint we are constantly being faced with possible life changing decisions and choices, it constantly appears that we can mess up our own life, or someone else's, or indeed the whole of creation! We can look back and say "if only I hadn't made that decision ten years ago everything would be different." It can be a model of regret, blame and missed opportunities.

The Non-dualistic view of a world based on Consciousness and precision is best summed up by Andrew Weil, MD, who suggested that mystical experience was the mirror image of negative paranoia. Paranoid persons believe there is a conspiracy in the universe against them while mystics believe there is a conspiracy in the universe in their favour.[1] I have to confess to accepting this view of the universe, not just because it seems a nice optimistic way of viewing life, but when I observe my life, there is a feeling of being looked after and of being carried. Things seem to work out in spite of me rather than because of me. There are far too many coincidences to be accounted for by accident, such as meeting people at just the right time and in a way that I could never have planned or anticipated. Then there are the many small things which happen that seem to have meaning; the way a book falls into my hands expressing just what I need to know at that time, maybe reflecting or reinforcing an experience I have just had or a line of thought I am developing.

Even people who have done me some apparent disservice or have taken some action definitely not motivated with my best interests at heart have, nonetheless, when seen from a distant vantage point, been playing an important role in my life and pushing me in the direction I had to go. So it seems, whether we like it or not, we are all actors in one great drama or dream, and that we are all knowingly or unknowingly playing necessary roles in each other's lives. The whole thing seems to dovetail together into one mysterious whole so that ultimately there is no blame for anybody, for we are all just parts of that whole and parts of that unfolding.

In the Indian traditions, there is the concept of Maya, which I find particularly helpful in trying to understand the Non-dual model. The word Maya has two meanings. Firstly, it is often used to describe the illusory nature of the entire manifest physical universe, subject to space and time, birth and death, creation, maintenance and destruction, and all the varied and changing dramas of our lives. But the word Maya also means the 'nature' or manifestation of the Divine Consciousness or God. So when we see the physical universe as a separate reality and everything in it as separate and mechanical then we are perceiving Maya in terms of illusion. But when we perceive the entire physical universe, including ourselves, not as a separate reality having its own existence, but as the nature or manifestation of the one Divine Consciousness, then we are experiencing Maya as the Nature of God.

There is a simile from the Upanishads that illustrates this point; in the darkness we see a coiled rope and mistake it for a snake and there is fear, but with light, the light of understanding, we see that it is not a snake but a piece of rope and all fear goes as we see its true nature. So from this viewpoint, although we perceive a separate external world that can at times appear quite frightening, the world is not what it appears to be. The rope, when looked at with understanding and a greater depth of vision, far from being a snake becomes our means of escape.

This concept of a conscious universe can be very difficult for the rational mind to accept, for it loves to think in terms of opposites: good and evil, truth and untruth, freewill or pre-ordination, etc.

In order to come close to understanding a universe that is all Consciousness, it is necessary to be able to live with two apparently contrary views at the same time and feel no contradiction. For myself this is the great paradox, learning to live with the 'both and'. For instance, the world is all Consciousness and is unfolding just as it should, and yet there is also a part to be played by individuals in introducing changes if that is their role. This happens because they are not something separate but are a part of that unfolding.

So it is quite possible to accept that everything is Consciousness and that there is no accident, and play a part in eradicating injustice, or introducing social reform, or a new paradigm in science, or in being passionate about both what we find unjust and also what delights us.

In this model as with the other models, there still arises the question of good and evil. If it is a Conscious universe why, when we look about us, is there so much that appears to be far from perfect? What is the role and purpose of suffering? Although we shall look at this question in more detail later, my answer would always have to be that "I do not know". I feel it is a mystery that is beyond the capacity of my rational mind to grasp and I would not presume to know the purpose of my own or any one else's life. It is almost as if that part of the mind that wants to work out the answers to everything, or the part of us that wants to be the one who 'knows', has to be suspended and we must just trust that everything is all right although it might sometimes appear to the contrary: I remember my own past experiences of suffering in life. How they always led to a period of new creativity or greater understanding or greater compassion. One answer to the question as to why something had to happen has to be, "The rest of your life will give you the answer."

In some of the eastern religions the concept of Good and Evil is not so clear cut as it has become in Christianity and Judaism, for example, where it seems to have become more of an objective concept. The concepts of good and bad can also have quite different meanings in relation to a particular aim. If my aim is just to become materially very wealthy, anything that takes me closer to that aim is 'good' and anything that takes me further away is 'bad'. Similarly if my aim is to grow in spiritual understanding and Universal compassion, then those things that bring me closer or move me further away from my goal, may not necessarily be the same as in the example of achieving material wealth.

As William Shakespeare observed in Hamlet:

There is nothing either good or bad, but thinking makes it so.

The myth of Adam and Eve from the Book of Genesis is interesting from this point of view. The expulsion from the Garden is about moving out of the undifferentiated Unity into the world of duality, separation and apparent opposites. You eat of the tree of the knowledge of good and evil and you start to experience everything as opposite and separate, man and woman, God and man, God and the world. Probably this is an inevitable part of being born into a physical world with a physical body. The return to the Garden is about going back into the Unity and transcending the world of opposites, not leaving them behind, but seeing that they are, in reality and from the largest viewpoint, all a part of the same thing. Thus the return to Paradise is not a question of literally going into another world where there are no opposites, but seeing this world from such a perspective that we start to experience everything as aspects of one mysterious whole so that it is not so much a question of where we look but of how we look.

In participating in life and saying 'yes' to its drama and its challenges, we may champion the side of 'good' and deplore the 'bad', but at the same time, be aware of a transcendent realm, beyond duality, from which this whole drama of life emanates. And perhaps this physical world is the one place where we really get the chance to practise seeing that, in all the varied experiences and difficulties we go through. It is in accepting this, that we integrate it into a larger whole and "return to the Garden."

Thus non-duality is not a state that the universe is evolving towards, rather the universe already is non-dual, so that it is not a question of bringing it into being, but rather of learning to look at the world and ourselves in a different way, as they already are though not necessarily how they may appear to us on the surface. I find it helpful to think of the One Consciousness as having two aspects: the still unmanifest Consciousness that is without change and the manifest nature of that Consciousness, the whole phenomenal universe that is subject to movement and change, birth and death, growth and decay.

In our daily lives it is important to attend to both these aspects of creation: to give attention to living in the world of manifestation and playing our parts in the drama of life, but also at the same time to be aware of the great stillness that is the Source and underlies all creation.

It is very easy to become totally involved with just the world of manifestation, with the drama, at the expense of the still unmanifest Consciousness. But, at certain moments, it is as if the curtain parts and we become aware of the underlying stillness. This can happen unexpectedly, often at moments of great happiness or even emergency or grief. The world loses its importance as the sole reality and we become aware of a deeper reality that is always present. We are no longer just caught up with the projected images on the screen, but become aware of the light of the projector.

This realisation can often come about as a result of the difficulties we experience in life, such as bereavement or illness. We are gradually brought to the realisation that there is more to life than we are experiencing with just our five senses. When this happens life takes on a very different quality; the drama of life is not seen as something separate but as all part of the manifest unfolding of the One Consciousness.

# CHAPTER 2

# THE FOUR LEVELS

In the different religious and philosophical traditions around the world the one Consciousness is often portrayed as manifesting itself in creation and in the individual through a series of levels. In the early Christian church the idea of three levels was introduced as Body, Soul and Spirit. This is a very helpful concept, as later in the church man has often been thought of as just body and soul, which means that God is somewhere outside, external and separate. But with the idea of body, soul and spirit the ground of our being and God are the same, for there is no separation at the level of spirit.

In the non-dualist Advaita tradition from India,

Consciousness is portrayed as manifesting through four levels: physical, subtle or psychological, causal and Divine. It is really the same as the Christian model, except that there is an additional sub division. The amount of information we want on each level varies from individual to individual at different times of life. Sometimes we want a great deal of information while at other times just a bare framework that we can carry around with us is all we need. In presenting this simple model of four levels it is important to realise that it is by no means definitive. In some traditions there is a much greater variety of levels and of sub divisions within each level. Indeed within different schools and traditions these same four levels are given different meaning and significance. So I am presenting it in its basic simplicity, in the way that I have understood and experienced it myself. For it is not the details that are important so much as the basic concept; there are not levels of Consciousness for Consciousness does not come in levels, there is nowhere that Consciousness is more or less. It is equally everywhere. Rather it is a question of levels of ignorance, or levels of mistaken identity.

On the individual scale the physical level is our physical body of flesh and bones, internal organs and neurochemical mechanisms, all observable and measurable by science. This level is subject to time and space, growth and decay.

The subtle or psychological level consists of our thoughts and feelings, desires and such aspects of mind as memory, discrimination and sense of I. This is the realm of individual experience that is known only to the individual. We can observe aspects of it manifesting in the physical body. For example, if I am very angry my face may become red or if I'm happy I may smile. If I am feeling compassionate my eyes will have a softness to them but if I am under attack my face and bodily posture may indicate fear.

The causal level or body is sometimes described as a formless realm of unmanifest potential. It is the level at which the light of pure Consciousness is reflected in the individual like the rays of the sun. The experience of that reflection varies according to the degree of transparency or opacity of the individual psyche just as a still and clear pond surface gives a brighter reflection of the sun. The causal body is also the level at which the whole of an individual's potential is stored in unmanifest form like an enfolded blueprint or coloured film, partly built up by the repetition of experience during childhood and subsequent life. All talents, experience and memory are contained here. There is no experience at this level, yet its content is manifest and experienced through the subtle and physical bodies. As with the analogy of a colour slide, what is seen on the screen is also on the slide.

The Divine body is the true Self, I or Consciousness that lies beyond the changing worlds of body, psychology, and potential, and yet which are a part of it and its vehicle for manifestation. At this level there is no separation between us or anyone else or the whole of creation. And these are not really separate levels or bodies, but each one is contained within the larger one, and is to some extent a partial or limited understanding of it.

In the Indian scripture, the Mandukya Upanishad, states of consciousness are described as corresponding to four levels. The daytime waking consciousness corresponds to the physical level, sleep with dreams to the subtle level, the deep sleep state to the causal level and the enlightened state to the Divine level. When we go to sleep at night, we withdraw our identification from the physical world and enter the subtle as we experience our own inner realm of dreams. From the subtle state to the causal we enter the state of dreamless sleep. This same process is reversed when we wake in the morning. It has been suggested in some traditions that this is also the process of birth and death. At birth we pass from the undifferentiated unity of the Divine level, through causal and subtle levels to the physical world. At death we shed our identity with the more finite levels and return to the unity of the Divine level.

These same four levels can be seen in the world around. The physical world is that world measurable and observable by science, from atomic particles to the vast physical universe of two hundred billion galaxies. The physical world that we see when we look around at the whole night sky is just a fraction of this vastness. This is contained within a subtle world of universal mind and universal memory, which again is contained within the casual world, a universal blueprint where all the laws of nature are in potential or enfolded. This is contained within One Universal Consciousness and the other levels are its manifestation and expression. In this model nothing is separate or outside of Consciousness. Consciousness is not in matter but matter is in Consciousness or, as the physicist David Bohm implied, the whole physical universe is a ripple on the surface of something so much vaster.

At times I have found it helpful to express this four-world concept in diagrammatic form, so that I can remember it, and use it as a simple framework to carry with me in my mind (see Fig 1).

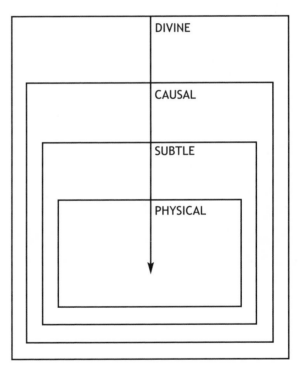

**Fig 1. The Model of the Four Worlds**

This model of four levels makes a very important framework for looking at all phenomena and all experience. Until we take into account the whole picture our deductions and conclusions will be incomplete. The true understanding of any phenomenon requires an understanding of all four levels though it should be remembered that confusion can arise from trying to understand one level with the logic of another level. For instance to understand the non dual nature of the Divine level when looking at the physical and subtle levels in isolation leads to confusion since these two levels are full of apparent opposites that must be contended with in daily life. It is easy to judge suffering from just the physical or psychological level without observing its possible transforming effect on the spiritual or Divine level.

In order to comprehend the non-dual nature of the universe it is not simply a matter of learning to see events from a larger physical perspective. This can be an attempt to quantify the higher levels with the cognition of the physical level when they are beyond physical qualification. Rather it is necessary for each individual to transform his or her perception so that events and phenomena are seen with the eye of Consciousness. This requires seeing in quite different categories because it is not just an alteration to rational thought.

This concept was understood by the Russian writer and philosopher P.D. Ouspensky. In the preface to his book, A New Model of the Universe he describes four different methods of observation and gives the analogy of a single room. The first method he calls the 'defective method' and it involves a glance at the room through the keyhole. The second or 'logical method' is based on a glance at the room from just one spot without enough light. The third or 'psychological method' involves walking around the room in daylight and examining the various objects in it. The fourth or 'esoteric method' includes not only the whole room with everything in it but also the occupations and relationships of all the people connected with it, the street that the house is in, its position in the town, the position of the town in the country, the country in relation to the earth, the earth within the solar system and so on. The esoteric method takes nothing in isolation but connects everything, no matter how small, with the whole.[2]

So for a complete understanding of any phenomenon it is necessary to understand it from the fullest point of view. Usually we just see cross sections or fragments of events and we base opinions and theories on a very limited amount of information. In much the same way we may look back at an event in our lives that seemed incomprehensible at the time, but from the vantage point of a greater perspective, its significance begins to become clear. A single event or meeting can often show the purpose and give meaning to a whole chain of previous events that at the time appeared to be the result of chance, accident or apparent 'mistakes'.

Thus what appears at the physical level to be accident or chance is, in the broader context of the causal level, cause and effect on too large a scale to observe. It is more than the physical keyhole view, but still not the whole picture, since a complete view includes the Divine level, which is the cause beyond all apparent causes. From this perspective individuals are not the 'doers' or initiators of events or causes, any more than a train creates a station it has not yet reached. From this perspective the entire universe on all levels is sometimes described as a drama or play unfolding in Consciousness.

The thirteenth-century Persian poet and mystic Jalalud-Din Rumi writing in his epic poem the Mathnawi tells a story that further illustrates this point. It tells of some ants who are on a piece of paper which is being written on by a pen. One ant says, "How wonderful it is that the pen can do this writing!" Another slightly wiser ant says: "No, it is not the pen that writes but the hand that holds it!" and another ant says, "No, it is not the hand but the arm that moves!" And so the ants go back in the causal chain until one ant "who is a little bit sagacious" says, "No, the writing is caused by the Universal Spirit that gives movement to all things."

This is a very helpful story for it is easy in our observation of events to stop far short of the original cause just as the ants did. I often find it necessary to be aware at any one time of more than one cause. There is the physical or psychological cause in space and time but simultaneously it is part of a great unfolding, the purpose of which I only dimly perceive or perhaps never understand.

So the concept of different levels can be a great help in understanding phenomena and resolving many of the paradoxes that exist when we collapse all our understanding to just one level. Much of the world's great religious and mystical teachings can be understood quite differently when looked at from the perspective of different levels. There is a traditional fable found in many different cultures that illustrates this point. It tells of how an elephant appeared in a village inhabited by blind men who, in order to find out what the elephant was like, all took hold of different parts of it. The one who held the trunk said, "the elephant is long and thin like a snake", whilst the one who touched a leg said, "no it is like a tree trunk" and the one who touched the belly said, "no it is large and round like a barrel". In this way the argument went on until a sighted man arrived who was able to put a stop to the quarrel by pointing out that what they were each describing was just a particular part of the elephant and that by putting all their understandings together they could produce a much fuller picture of the whole elephant.

I feel that the model of a Universal Consciousness manifesting through a series of levels is very similar to this. We tend to try to understand the whole picture from the viewpoint of just one level and then quarrel with others who are seeing it from another level, without realising that these are all just different perspectives of the same thing and that the most complete view includes all levels.

This model also has great practical implications for how we learn to integrate the varied experiences in our lives into a greater whole. From the fullest Divine perspective the universe is unfolding just as it should down to the smallest detail, but from the much narrower keyhole view which I usually have of events, they often seem far from perfect and seem to unfold in a very different way according to how my separate ego self would like things to be. Consequently the nature of the unfolding of the Universal Consciousness can seem paradoxical and against all logic, not because in reality it is so, but because that is how it can appear as a result of trying to understand events from a more limited level of cognition. There have been many times in my life where a relationship has not worked out, or has not happened at all, where a particular job of work I wanted has not materialised or an illness has developed causing a total change in life direction and a need to drop all plans. Yet nearly always, when I later view the events from a distance in time, I get a hint as to why things worked out that way. I can see that a particular relationship was totally unsuitable and just based on my projection. The job would never have suited me and there was a much better one waiting.

There is an old Greek folk tale that illustrates this same process of how difficult it is to judge the events of our lives in isolation, without seeing the whole picture. The story tells of a girl called Latifa who was the daughter of a prosperous spinner. One day, while she was travelling near Crete with her father, their ship was wrecked and she was washed up on the shore quite destitute. She was eventually found by a family of cloth makers who took her into their home and taught her their craft and she became quite happy with her lot. One day, however, when she was on the seashore, she was kidnapped by a band of slave traders and sold into slavery in Istanbul. Her world had collapsed for a second time. She was bought by a man who made masts for ships. She worked hard for him and learned the art of making masts. And so Latifa became happy in her third career.

One day she had to go with a cargo of ship's masts to Java, but the ship was wrecked by a hurricane off the coast of China where Latifa was washed ashore. Once again her world had collapsed and she cursed her fate wondering why all these unfortunate things happened to her.

Now it so happened that there was a legend in China that one day a woman would arrive who would be able to make a tent for the Emperor as nobody in China could make tents. When Latifa was washed ashore it was the time when heralds travelled around China to see if any strangers had arrived who could make a tent. So Latifa was taken before the Emperor. "Can you make a tent?" he asked her. "I think so," she said.

She asked for rope but there was none. Remembering her time as a spinner she made rope from flax. She asked for stout cloth but there was none. Remembering her time as a cloth maker she was able to make stout tent cloth. Then she needed tent poles but there were none in China so remembering her time as a maker of ship's masts she made tent poles and remembering all the tents she had seen on her travels, she made a tent.

The Emperor was so pleased that he offered Latifa the fulfilment of any wish. She chose to stay in China where she married a handsome prince and lived in happiness till the end of her days. Thus Latifa realised that what appeared to be ill-fortune was actually a necessary stage in finding her true happiness.

In taking a broad view of life and learning to trust in its process I feel that it is important that we do not use this view to deny the validity of our day to day experiences and emotions. It is easy to use our belief systems as a means of keeping life at a distance. We can end up very spiritually 'top heavy' but with no trust in life and its unfolding, when our spiritual life and life in the world are mistakenly seen as separate. When we confront aspects of our emotional or physical life that may have become outlived or belong to an earlier stage of our development, we may hide behind religious belief and doctrine as a means of avoidance rather than integration into a larger whole and wider sphere of being. It is important that as each level or stage is transcended it must then be integrated into the one above. So it is necessary to attend to each level equally and not say, "Oh, that's just the physical side or life" or "it's just psychology" for all, equally, are manifestations of the Divine. When necessary aspects of experience at these different levels are 'by-passed' or missed out they can emerge later as symptoms or repetitive situations demanding that we attend to some aspect of the physical or psychological in our lives so that we arrive at a fuller integration.

In the same way in some traditions there is a tendency to dismiss the rational mind; it is transcended and then dismissed. But it is very important that rationality is not dismissed but is integrated into the deeper levels and is enriched by them, for it is an important function of Consciousness and is an important tool to use in coming to understand ourselves and the universe.

So the model of four worlds gives us a simple picture of how Spirit or Consciousness manifests as a material creation and also shows us a different way of looking both at that world and at the events in it. It shows the importance of not judging it from too narrow a view but rather from as  wide a perspective as possible and not just a wider perspective in time and space, but from a point of view of its depth in the 'Now'.

# CHAPTER 3

# WHO AM I?

We have all at different times found it necessary to question the nature of our own existence and ask the question "Who am I?" Am I just a physical body containing a brain? Are all my talents, experiences, perceptions and peculiarities just the result of brain function alone? Are all my emotions, hopes, aspirations and creativity only the result of brain function or is there something else? Am I something more than just a mechanical body-mind reacting to external stimuli?

The death of a relative or loved one in particular can make us question the sense of our own identity as we ask, "but where are they now?" It is a shock when someone who was so vital, alive and individual is suddenly no longer present. It feels impossible that they can just disappear, just as it seems impossible that we ourselves can disappear. When I was a child I often wondered where I was a few years before I was born. I would ask myself, "What is this sense of individuality? Why am I me and not someone else? Is there more to me than I normally experience? Why at times do I feel so much more alive and so much more myself than at other times?"

When I look back at life, in many ways I feel a totally different person from myself as a child or as a teenager because I have had so much more experience of life and many of my interests and views and my physical appearance have changed. Yet there is also a part of me that stays exactly the same regardless of age, status, health or interests. In a strange way, the fundamental feeling of 'I' is just the same. It's not the part of me that thinks or feels or reacts to life's events or a part that I can separate from and observe, but rather it feels much more like a basic sense of 'I' that stands in the background observing and witnessing all the changes of mood that go on within my psychology and the changing situations that go on within my life, yet all without comment or judgement.

Many of the world's religious and philosophical systems teach the importance of the transformation of our ordinary sense of 'I' or ego. Yet this concept is also easily misunderstood and can lead to an artificial suppression of our own very important sense of 'I' and sense of identity. A sense of pride in ourselves and in our achievements is very important and loss of a normal healthy sense of 'I' can be the start of mental illness. As we grow up it is important to develop a healthy sense of ego and identity. Attempts to curb this artificially can result in a false sense of modesty or humbleness, and a suppression of our natural liveliness.

With regard to the question, "Who am I?" I find it helpful to use the model of the four worlds to see with which body we identify. I can say 'I' to my physical body but I find this is always changing. It is subject to disease and decay, parts of it can even be removed, and in the end it returns back into the elements from which it came. Can the body really be regarded as a permanent sense of 'I'?

I can say 'I' to my subtle body or psyche but this too is in a state of constant change. At this level we are rather like a large and varied cast of theatrical characters who, at any minute, can take on a different character becoming centre stage and claiming to be 'I'. At this level, as we grow so we develop different characters according to our circumstances. I know just from observing myself that I tend to vary quite a lot at this level as I can't predict who I will be in a given situation. While I may be quite certain at a given time that a course of action is definitely the right thing to do, later I think, "My God, why on earth did I do or say that?" It's a good thing to recognise in yourself, because the more you can see it in yourself and acknowledge it, the more you can understand and accept it in others; at the level of the psyche there is little permanence.

Similarly the causal body, while it contains an enfolded blueprint of potential and is the realm in which the light of pure Consciousness is reflected in the individual, is still subject to modification and change, and so cannot be said to be the ultimate source of our sense of 'I'.

At the level of the Divine body there is no sense of change or impermanence. It is always the same. The experience of it may fluctuate but that is due to the changeable nature of the other levels. So it is this level to which we can say 'I' and this is the basis of our unchanging sense of 'I' that observes the fluctuations in our nature. So to return to the concept of ego, it is surely more a question of mistaken identity. It is possible to have a very narrow and limited sense of 'I' if we identify with just body, mind or potential as separate entities. We can identify with our real deeper Selves as part of a larger whole and from this point of view we are not all separate entities but all part of one great unfolding. This deep sense of 'I' is that same Witness that alone stands in the background and observes without comment what goes on in the worlds of body and psychology. It is not something we create or even something we uncover. It is always present whether we are aware of it or not. To become aware of it we simply transfer our attention from that which is seen to that which is the seer or Witness. It is only a question of acknowledging what already is. Gradually the Witness can be experienced as separate from our psychological mechanisms. We start to see that those aspects of our psyche that had previously driven us into action, and with which we had identified, are not ultimately our true Selves. When we identify with that which can be observed we are in the world of time, of change and becoming. This is what Joseph Campbell called the tick of time which shuts out the knowledge of eternity.[3] While we identify with the field of time we are subject to the dualities of past and future, good and bad. When we withdraw from identification with what is seen and acknowledge the 'seer' we move beyond the field of time and into the 'Now'. So to acknowledge our identity with this ever-present witness, we take ourselves back in the causal chain until what we are left with is our own basic awareness that is our true Self and is Reality all at once.

When we practise methods such as meditation our sense of self is transferred back through the different levels. We gradually shed our sole identity with the physical world of sense perception and then let go of our sole identity with the subtle world of thoughts, feelings and desires until we enter the causal world of no experience. It is a state of 'objectless awareness'. The analogy is sometimes used of a projector running but with no film. The light of Consciousness shines but with no object of awareness.

In the Advaita tradition this state is known as samadhi. We all enter the causal realm of no experience unconsciously at night in deep sleep. It is also available during the day between the end of one set of desires and the start of another set, when we can naturally rest at this silent awareness.

As this experience deepens we find that we are no longer so identified with the drama of life. We become like an actor who plays his role as best he can but who never forgets who he really is, in the same way that we might view a film at the cinema. You are aware of your identity as the still impartial

Witness and your exclusive identity with the mind-body mechanism has been dropped.

There are moments when the moving mind becomes quiet and we feel our identity as deep stillness. Life goes on just the same yet we are able to observe it without quite the same feeling of involvement, almost as if it is all happening to someone else. The mind and body responds to each situation as it arises in the moment but without being coloured by the usual prejudices and preconceptions.

Paradoxically, at such times, far from becoming remote and distant life becomes more alive, colours are more vivid, we are more aware of sounds, smells and sense perceptions in general. Also we have more empathy for the needs of others and understand what the necessary action is for each situation. We begin to become aware of this ever-present Witness when we start to view our lives as part of a drama, all unfolding in Consciousness. When this happens the ego's need to manipulate its surroundings lessens and our sense of identity automatically begins to shift from its sole identity with the mind-body mechanism at the subtle and physical level to that of the Observer or Witness at the causal and Divine levels. We begin to watch our lives unfold with the curiosity of an interested observer. It becomes more a question of, "I wonder what happens next" rather than, "I wonder what I should do next".

In the non-dual traditions the analogy of a mirror is often used to describe this state. We simply reflect, without comment, all that arises.

We sometimes receive unexpected glimpses of this deep,

universal sense of 'I' at moments of emergency or great grief when it is almost as if the curtains part for a while and we are in the presence of something that is awesome, all knowing, full of love, very familiar, as if it's something we have known and wanted all our lives, and yet at the same time is 'I', who we really are.

At different times in our lives, particularly in childhood, we can get glimpses of this deep Self. It always brings a strange feeling of happiness, often for no discernible reason in the outside world. Indeed it seems that a deep sense of happiness not dependent on external circumstances is one of the touchstones by which to recognise the experience of this sense of Self. There is a sense of always having known it and having always been searching for it and that we have often seen its reflection in the things we desire and the things we think will bring us happiness. We've sought its reflection and recognised its dim memory in this person and that person, in the distance beyond a hazy range of hills on a midsummer evening, in the early morning mist on a river in autumn, and yet here it is all the time, who we really are; the ground of our being. Perhaps it manifests at unusual and unexpected times because that is when our psychology is often quietened and when we become still and transparent. Then it can shine right through our being as if it is really just seeing itSelf reflected in the world around; Self recognises Self with nothing in between.

I remember the night before my mother's funeral, we had asked if her coffin could be left in the church over night so that my brother and sister and I could meditate for half an hour by it the night before. It had been an unexpected death, and my grief was at its height, full and all consuming. At first it was very difficult to become quiet, but then towards the end of the half-hour I became full of strange inner happiness. I could feel it welling up from within. It felt like a communication with my Self, which at the same time was my mother's Self and was beyond death and beyond all harm. I left the church feeling so happy and knowing that everything was all right. In the ground of our being it really is all right and we really are all one. Later that evening a friend rang to see how I was feeling and I think she was rather puzzled that I felt so happy in the circumstances. That feeling carried me through the funeral and beyond.

It is extraordinary that we all have this Self that lies beyond our day-to-day psychology, that is our birthright and the person we really are, and yet so often we remain unaware of its existence. It does appear that there are two stages to its realisation. The first is going inwards in stillness to discover this Self within, like a safe place of no fear and great confidence that observes the world and the changes within our own psychology without comment, and from which emanates a great deal of happiness. If we stop at this point we are still in a world of duality. There may be a safe place within but there is still a separate outer world. There is still the experience of subject and object, or duality. So the second stage involves realising that this Self is not separate but is the same as everybody else's true Self and is also the Self of the whole universe. Whether we look inside ourselves or outside it is still the same Self that we are experiencing since there is no place where it is lacking or absent and there is no longer a division into subject and object or seer and seen. In this second stage, because there is not the separation between the witness and what is being witnessed, events are not judged by a separate sense of ego and so are not categorised into dualities such as good or bad, but are seen as they are - all aspects of one unity.

There is an Indian tale that illustrates the fact that for the person who is fully awakened to the non-dual Reality, God is perceived as doing everything:

A certain monk from a local monastery was out begging for food when he saw a Landlord mercilessly beating a man. The monk pleaded with the Landlord to stop, but he was so filled with anger, that he turned his fury upon the monk, until he was left unconscious on the ground. Soon he was found by his fellow monks who carried him back to the monastery and nursed his wounds. They all sat round him tending to his needs, until one suggested that he should be given a little milk. When it was poured into his mouth he regained consciousness and looked around. In order to test that he was indeed conscious one of the monks shouted in his ear: "Reverend sir, who is giving you milk?" "Brother", replied the injured monk in a low voice, "he who beat me is now giving me milk."

In the different religious and philosophical traditions the true Self is given different names: in Buddhism, especially as it comes from Tibet, and in the Zen schools of Japan it is called the Buddha Nature or Nature Mind. In the Vedic scriptures of Hinduism it is called the Atman or Divine Self, that is of the same nature as the Param Atman or Self of the Universe. I suspect that there is not in reality an individual Divine Self and a Universal Divine Self. We have the experience or sensation of an individual Divine Self when the light of the Universal is reflected in the deeper levels of our own individual psyches, but when the Universal is directly experienced as Self we are no longer contained within our normal boundaries and the whole Universe is experienced as internal rather than external.

In many of the different scriptures the Divine Self is personified. For example in the Bhagavad Gita of Vyasa that forms a part of the great epic, The Mahabharata, Krishna is a personification of the cosmic person or Self. So it is not a story about a real historical person but a symbol of this universal truth or reality. I feel that in the Gospels the image of Jesus is often used in the same way. For example, when he says "No one comes to the Father except through me!", a verse that is often used by fundamentalists to warn unbelievers that they are on the wrong path, it does not literally mean that unless everyone is Christian they will not go to Heaven. Rather it is first necessary to go inwards to discover your own deep Self in order to realise your already existing unity with the whole of creation.

Thus, from the view of our deeper Selves, there is no such thing as a material world on the one hand and a spiritual world on the other, for it is all perceived as a spiritual world. The duality of matter and Spirit is caused by our own perception and the level of ourselves with which we identify.

In both Buddhist and Hindu thought there is another aspect to the concept of 'I' and our feeling of separation and this is the concept of samskara. As we go through life, especially in early childhood, we pick up certain habits. We learn ways of reacting to the world and situations, we find that certain ways of reacting help us to get our own way or get our needs met. We may use certain modes of behaviour to avoid pain or a painful situation. Later the painful situation no longer exists and yet our learnt response remains, emerging whenever we are in a similar situation. It is partly these deeply ingrained tendencies that go to make up our samskara, residing in the causal body, and the light of Consciousness, who we really are, filters through and is coloured by this layer of individuality.

Because it is deep in our nature, we are mostly unaware of its existence. We only sometimes get glimpses of it if we are very honest in looking at ourselves, or we may see it reflected in those aspects of others that we find difficult. It feels to me as if it is in layers of strata and it is possible at one time to see so much and then gradually we see more and more. There is no good or bad involved in this concept, although in one sense it may obstruct the natural brilliancy of our real Selves, yet without it there would be no drama of life and no unfolding and no journey of Self discovery. It is this that gives us our grist for the mill.

There are many different stories in mythology that tell of quests to find treasure or journeys to meet a monarch who has offered to give up his kingdom at a particular time, yet on the way there are all sorts of attractions to which many succumb so that very few actually complete the quest.

These stories are often told in India to emphasise the importance of going direct to the Source and not being content to settle for lesser levels of identity. It also warns against the attractions of yogic powers or siddhis and the psychic no man's land that can end up strengthening our sense of separation rather than dissolving it. The subtle level, although a part of the manifestation of Consciousness, when taken in isolation can become a great barrier and limitation. It is a very attractive world of images and dreams, a domain of separation, which on its own cannot be fully trusted. I find it is always necessary to go beyond it to the stillness and fullness of the causal and Divine levels, to one's own true Self, the part that alone knows what is the right thing for the individual in any situation and from which emanates a deep wordless assurance. It is necessary to remember that it is not simply achieving a higher state of consciousness that is important, so much as acknowledging our already existing identity with our true Self that is the impartial witness of all the changing states we experience as well as the whole drama of our lives.

# CHAPTER 4

# BEING AND THE PRESENT MOMENT

Our most basic sense of identity is the feeling of "I am" or "I exist" and yet we have seen how we limit this identity to the vehicle of Consciousness rather than the Consciousness itself. We might say, "I am my body and psyche" or "I am tall" or "I am short" or "I am an artist or a doctor" and so on.

The seventeenth-century philosopher René Descartes helped limit our sense of identity with his famous dictum, "I think therefore I am", equating our identity with just the thinking aspect of the subtle body or psyche. But when we realise that there is also an aspect of ourselves that is aware that we are thinking, that silently observes the thinking and feeling processes, we see that consciousness is far more than just thought.

Perhaps the Book of Exodus in the Bible gives a more accurate image of our identity when God says to Moses from the burning bush, "I AM THAT I AM". Here there is no need to limit the feeling of 'I am' to any sort of identity. It is just a pure sense of 'Amness' without qualification, the same for each individual. "I am so and so" relates to our identity at the level of the ever changing drama of life. Our basic sense of "I AM" is beyond the changes of the mind and body, it is not only the "I AM" of every living creature, but also the "I AM" of spiral nebulae and galactic clusters. So that creation exists and unfolds within this sense of "Amness".

There is a concept found particularly in Zen Buddhism that is not really found in the West and that is the 'Isness' of a thing or person. It is also sometimes called Being or Presence. It is quite distinct from what people may know, where they have been, or what they have done in their lives.

Although it is difficult to describe, one can observe that there are some people who have more of a sense of 'Isness' than others. Such people are more present, more 'behind their eyes'. They may have quite frail physical bodies and yet something seems to emanate from them. It is not just a physical vitality but a quality of light and warmth and humour. This is not only the domain of great saints or holy men. It can be seen in the most unusual circumstances and people. Sometimes people show this quality not long before they die as if part of them is already aware of a greater reality, or the part of their psyche that obscures it is no longer so opaque. Others develop it much earlier on in life.

I think that this quality of Being is the degree to which we let the light of our true Selves shine through our natures. It is the degree to which we have become transparent. For some the concept of our deepest Self, or sense of Identity being Universal is difficult. It is an attack against our sense of individuality, in the same way that the idea of a non-dual universe can be a threat to a separate sense of ego that may have built much of the reason for its existence on the illusory notion of saving the world. But really any fear of not existing, or of losing one's individuality, is not a fear at all. In a small sense our existence is just like a dirty bit of glass not letting the light pass through. When the glass is a bit cleaner, if only momentarily, one both exists and does not exist. One becomes a vehicle for the transmission of light because the real joy is not so much feeling happy in a personal way but becoming aware of an immense force flowing through one and outwards towards others and all creation.

There is a great key to the experience of our true Being or 'I AM' and that is that it only exists in the present moment. It is mainly uncontrolled thinking that makes us unaware of it. We tend to live a greater part of our lives in either regret and memory of the past or anticipation and fear of the future. Yet both of these actually do not exist. The only thing that exists is the eternal present. When we silently rest in the present, our connection with a separate self supported by the memory of passing time dissolves and we become aware of a much larger presence that exists only in the now.

One of the ways I find most effective for coming into the present is that when my mind has taken me off into the past and I am experiencing regret, anger or sadness, or when it is in the future and I experience fear or anxiety, is to ask, "But what is wrong now?" Nearly always nothing is wrong at this moment and I am flooded with a feeling of warmth and presence that my mind-identified state was causing me to miss. Fears about a possible future or regrets about the past only exist when we allow our minds to move away from the present. And even if an anticipated future situation does turn out to have some basis in reality, we actually experience the event in the present very differently from the way we anticipated it. Winston Churchill once quoted an old man as saying on his deathbed, "I've had a lot of trouble in my life most of which never happened."

One of the chief indicators of not being in tune with our true Being in the present moment is fear. Fear is purely a product of our psyche, or the psyche when taken in isolation. When we are in tune with our true Selves we have a feeling of deep confidence in the process of life's unfolding, even if our lives may not be particularly easy, or our way forward very clear. Nonetheless at the back of our minds there is the feeling that everything is all right and just as it should be. Perhaps this is because the real Self is outside of time and space and already knows the outcome of the particular life process that we are in, and that we are being lovingly led and looked after.

When we look at it closely it becomes apparent that so much of what we find difficult in human behaviour has its origin in fear, and so many of the difficulties in our own lives stem from fear in its various forms. If someone is behaving in an unpleasant, aggressive or bullying manner, such behaviour rarely if ever comes out of a psyche that is confident, happy and balanced. When we are happy and content within ourselves, we are usually outwardly loving and accepting of those around us. The bully bullies others because he is insecure and fearful within him or herself. People who are always boasting about their achievements or conquests or their material wealth only do so not because they really are full of confidence and think themselves better than everybody else, but because they are insecure and hence need to put on a show in order to boost their low self esteem, at least to themselves if not anybody else. Fundamentalists cling tightly to rigid outer forms and definitions and often take offence when criticised, not because they are certain that their view alone is right but because deep down they are fearful and uncertain, and having a rigid framework or set of rules can bring some security. Criticism becomes intolerable because it threatens to undermine what is a very insecure and shaky structure that is not necessarily built on the foundations of deep inner experience.

The experience of fear at the subtle level is also significant to the way we view the world about us, and how we perceive other people. Seeing ourselves as separate can also bring with it the feeling that the world about us is external and potentially hostile. And it is easy to project our own fears and insecurities onto those around us. We may react in hurt or anger to an innocent comment from someone, not because it was intended to hurt us, but because it touched a layer of insecurity and fear within us. In the same way an innocent remark of ours can spark off an unexpected reaction from another when it touches a layer of damage of which we may have been totally unaware.

I find this point of view very helpful in learning to accept the sometimes inexplicable behaviour of others, and indeed my own strange behaviour at times. The understanding that deep insecurity is so often at the root of aggressive and unpleasant behaviour allows me to have more compassion for the other person and hence tailor my reaction accordingly. I am also helped in this by the understanding that the things I react to or find difficult in others, are almost always aspects of my own character that I am seeing reflected in them, as if we act as mirrors to each other. I have noticed both with myself and with others that we usually suspect other people of doing the things that we ourselves are potentially capable of. If not the thought just never occurs to us, that a person could or would do such a thing. Thus it is often said that criticism tells you more about the person who is doing the criticising, than about the one criticised.

So a part of becoming transparent and reflecting who we really are at a deep level also involves having a transparent truthfulness with ourselves at the subtle level, so that the particular unacceptable aspects of ourselves that we project onto others can be acknowledged and then integrated into a larger whole. In keeping with a non-dual model, where everything is a part of that whole, fear has its place. It plays an important role in our lives. Without it we might get into all sorts of trouble and it can also act as an indicator that we are out of touch with ourSelves and be used to guide us back to our centre. Whenever I experience fear or anxiety I am aware that I have forgotten that my life is part of a perfectly unfolding drama, and I can then use the experience to take me back to my place of no fear.

Another indicator of our true Being is that it cannot be observed as it is itSelf the Observer. When we identify our sense of Self with anything that can be observed then it is subject to change and ultimately suffering. So all these different changing thoughts and feelings that pass through our consciousness like clouds in the sky can be reminders to acknowledge our true 'I am' that is always present and is beyond change.

# CHAPTER 5

# THE CIRCLE OF LIFE

In his poem, the Mathnawi, Rumi tells a lovely story about a man who lived in Baghdad and dreamt that there was a great treasure in a certain house in Cairo. The man set out and after many trials and tribulations reached the house in Cairo he had dreamt about. All he found there was a man who said, "That's funny, I keep dreaming there's a great treasure in a certain house in Baghdad." The man recognised this as his own house. So he returned to his house and sure enough found the treasure.

The moral of this story, as I understand it, is that although we already have the greatest treasure within us it is necessary to leave it in a metaphorical way, and to go out into life and to have all sorts of varied experiences in order to discover that we have always possessed this great treasure and have never been separate from it. So we rediscover it in a much fuller way than if we had not been separated from it in the first place. And it is only in setting out on the journey and saying 'yes' to the experience of life that we find it.

This is of course the same story as the parable of the prodigal son from St Luke's Gospel where a man leaves his father's house and goes out into the world until eventually he is reduced to eating the husks of the food fed to the pigs. Then he "comes unto himself" and begins the return to his father's house and his father sees him from afar and runs out to meet him. People are often a bit puzzled as to why he then gets treated to a big party by the father, whereas the other son who stayed at home gets no party. But, as we have seen, it is in making the journey of life that we rediscover this principle of Consciousness in a much fuller way than if we had never made the journey in the first place.

I can understand this a little from my own experience, for in my own journey through life I have often reached a plateau of comparative happiness and contentment and I've thought to myself, "Yes, life is really good." But then comes a very difficult patch and all the happiness and contentment is lost. Later, when the difficulty is past and I return to a happy state, it seems to have a much greater depth and fullness to it than the first state, which now appears quite limited by comparison. This is a continuing process like an ongoing initiation into finer and deeper levels of my being. The importance of stepping out into the drama of life is that it allows this process to happen.

So I find it strange when people separate living a full life in the world from the idea of Self-discovery or development. For myself the two are inseparably bound up together. Indeed each person's life seems to be his own route to this realisation, like a special individual course in yoga. It feels as if each person is led along a definite pathway with specific experiences that have to be gone through and assimilated and integrated into a larger whole, almost as if we set out on this journey with a particular puzzle to solve or an illusion to be dissolved.

It is often acknowledge that when people first set out on a particular spiritual path they receive a lot of quite intense experiences like a sort of honeymoon period. But later as they progress these experiences can become few and far between, and it is necessary for the aspirant to depend on his or her own inner reserve and trust even if the way forward is not always clear. This can cause people continually to seek new paths just to have the honeymoon period again and again, but if they persist, later, as the journey nears its end, they see that the guidance was never lacking and they were never separate from it.

There is a further paradox. If we remember that the true Self is already fully present as our ground awareness and consciousness, then when we set out to try to 'realise' it we immediately disengage from it, at least in memory and acknowledgement, and set off on a journey in the field of time where it is definitely not to be found until we discover that we have had it all along, as in the concept from Zen of the Gateless Gate. We may spend all our lives struggling to get through a particular gate, but once we are through it and look back we may ask whether there was really any gate to get through or, indeed, anyone to get through it?

One of the most direct ways to the realisation of our true Selves is through developing our talents and the things we love and playing our own role in the drama of life.

So how do we discover for ourselves what our life's purpose is? I find that I sometimes have a sense of being in co-operation with my life, of accepting and adapting to its changing circumstances. At other times I am in opposition to it or try to force and manipulate it to go my way, or the way my ego thinks it ought to go. There is an old Chinese Taoist concept called Wu-Wei. Wu Wei is to do with being sensitive to the nature and flow of things, not in opposition to events. There is a simile used in the martial arts in the East that when a strong wind blows, a pine tree stands rigidly against it, and ultimately gets blown over whereas bamboo bends before the wind, and then ultimately springs up again.

We create separation when we start resisting the flow and direction of our life and want the world to be other than it is. In doing this we disconnect from the universal and the present moment 'now' as it is. Our ego or psychology says, "I don't want that to happen, I want this to happen", and at that moment we are shut off by our psychology from our connection with the whole picture, and we become separate and opposed to the way things are.

This is not in anyway advocating passivity, for in entering into the drama of life, we act it out to the full, as in the fable of the two frogs who fell into a bowl of milk. The lazy frog said, "We're lost", and he sank to the bottom and drowned, but the other frog went on kicking and kicking until eventually the milk turned into butter and out he hopped.

In achieving our life's goals it is often necessary to exhaust ourselves again and again and to persist. Also at the back of our minds is the thought, "but who is really doing all this? Am I as a small self really the doer of my actions and the creator of my life?" For example, when I paint a picture or design a textile or write something, although there are years of experience, lots of research and a great deal of effort going into its execution, when it's done I think, "Gosh where did that come from?" It seems as if somehow the painting or design was already there in the big picture and has nothing to do with me as an individual. I just feel in a strange way like I am a vehicle for its expression.

The American mythologist and writer Joseph Campbell used to teach at Sarah Lawrence College in New York. Sometimes his students would come to him not sure what subjects or career path to follow, saying that their father wanted them to study law, or their mother wanted them to be a doctor, and suddenly while they were talking they would hit on a subject that they really responded to and their eyes would open and their complexion change, and if they had the courage to follow that, and hang onto it, even if it meant years of hard work and little money, then they had found their life right there. And Joseph Campbell called this, "following your Bliss", having the courage to follow that deep sense of rightness wherever it leads you, and not to be put off by the setbacks, but still to go on and persist.

He felt that when you do "follow your Bliss" you put yourself on a sort of track in life that had been there all the while waiting for you, that the life you were living was the one you were meant to be living, then you would meet people who were in "the field of your Bliss" and doors would open for you where you did not know they were going to be.[3]

I have found this to be very much my own experience, though it is also necessary to be awake to the moment when a particular path in life has played its role and comes to an end, and so be prepared to let go of what may have been our bliss in the past.

It is important to respond to our inner need to follow our own path and to trust where it is leading us, to trust the process of life and its unfolding. This is not always easy due to the expectations and judgements of others and it can sometimes take much courage. If we take action just to please an authority figure in our lives, we may come to regret it years later and realise we are not the person we wanted to be.

So it is necessary to be true to oneSelf, and to follow one's own inner light and where it leads. No one really knows what is right for another person; only that person knows and then often only from moment to moment. When we are really being ourSelves, then automatically we are playing our own role in the big drama of life, or our note in the symphony. We are doing what we are here for, and often it does not have to be anything world changing and dramatic

- just being oneself is enough. In a strange way when we are really being ourSelves we inspire others to be likewise.

I think we do not fully understand the effect we have on other people or that they can have on us, or the different roles we may have to play in relation to them. It can often be the smallest contact or gesture that we have made with someone in passing, perhaps just a smile or remark, that is in some way pivotal in their day or week or life.

Because life does appear to be a very precise drama and a strange web of interconnections, I have noticed how the purpose of events, or apparently chance meetings, often do not become clear until years later, when this person or that event may have a crucial role to play. I often look back and think, "Fancy that person playing that role in my life. I would never have suspected it when we first met briefly all those years ago." I have often observed this with people who later on become partners. It is as though when they first meet one or both of them is not yet ready and they have to go through various life experiences quite independently of each other before they are ready, and then they meet again, years later, sometimes almost a whole lifetime later. I can think of several occasions where I've met someone and I thought, "but I'm sure I know you, or am meant to know you" and much later their circumstances have changed and we have become great friends. So again it is as if at a deep level a part of us is vaguely aware of the script of our lives. Perhaps it is because our real Self, who we really are, is outside the ordinary confines of time and space and does indeed know the whole story.

Sir Laurens van der Post gave a remarkable illustration from his life of how an apparently small and insignificant event can have major implications later on. It was when he was a young journalist in Pretoria and he was in a café having coffee and waffles when he heard a great commotion. He saw that the lady who owned the café was shouting at two oriental gentleman, "Get out, I can't have niggers in this place." The two men were dumfounded so Laurens van der Post went over to them and asked, "Would you two gentlemen do me the honour of coming and having a cup of tea with me?" They turned out to be two of the most distinguished Japanese correspondents and as a result of this incident he was able to help them with their work. They became friends and later he was invited to Japan at the expense of the Japanese government.

Many years later during the Second World War he was on patrol with his men when he suddenly walked into a Japanese ambush, and the Japanese soldiers were coming at him from all sides. Then suddenly from far back came the Japanese that he had learnt long ago on his way to Japan by ship. There are many degrees of politeness in Japan, and the highest degree occurred to him. He held out his hand and called out as loudly as he could, "Would you please be so kind as to condescend to wait an honourable moment." The Japanese soldiers who were expecting to be shot at were not prepared for such a high degree of politeness so the potentially lethal situation was diffused, and Sir Laurens van der Post and his men were taken prisoner. The interesting thing that flashed through his mind at that moment was that all those years ago in Pretoria when he interrupted and invited the two Japanese men to sit at his table, he was saving his own life that morning on the mountain, and it became a tremendously important parable for him.[4]

When we start to notice this strange synchronicity in our lives it should not come as such a surprise. From the point of view of the non-dual model it is not a question of a myriad separate individuals interacting with each other but rather facets of the One Mind or One Consciousness interacting with itSelf.

This leads on to a question that is often asked, about which people hold very strong opinions, "Is there free will or is everything pre-ordained? Is our life-path already fully in existence or do we create it moment by moment?" From the point of view of the non-dual model I feel it is neither of these since free will and pre-ordination are one of the pairs of opposites that non-duality transcends. And this is surely an example of trying to solve a problem with the mind that is beyond rational explanation. I do feel, however, from observation, that my life appears to be following a well-written script and I am gradually learning to trust it rather than fight it.

So it does look very much as if I'm acting out a set role or being led along a set path of experience, in order to learn certain things, and come closer to discovering who I really am, and the true nature of Reality. Is there really anything so very wrong or difficult about the idea of one's life being planned by a Universal Consciousness, that has one's best interests at heart? I find it an immensely reassuring idea. I cause myself pain when I want it to be other than it is meant to be. I want that job, or that girlfriend or that house. But then the wanting and wandering and disappointments are surely all a part of the experience, and I am able to return to my path and think: "Oh well, that person, or job, or house just wasn't on my blueprint after all, but something more suitable will be", and I am able to carry onwards with trust.

In his autobiography, Memories, Dreams, Reflections Carl Jung also expresses the idea that his life had been assigned to him by fate and had to be fulfilled and this gave him an inner certainty. He did not have this certainty. It had him, and nobody could rob him of the conviction that it was enjoined upon him to do what God wanted and not what he wanted.[5]

I have often seen in my own life that it was not so much a question of my wanting to do something but rather that "this is something I am meant to do".

This outlook also has an advantage in that it allows me to take risks, not the sort of risks that involve jumping in front of London buses or walking over cliff tops, but the sort of risks that allow me to test my 'blueprint' and see if a certain direction is the right one, by going down it. If it is not, it soon closes up and I am returned to my true path, for it is in my experience impossible to go down a wrong avenue in life. There is a traditional Indian fable that illustrates the principle of testing one's 'blueprint' and how it is sometimes necessary to explore and make mistakes. It tells of how when cows are let out into the pasture in the spring time, all the cows and their calves become mixed up, so in order to find its right mother the calf goes from cow to cow giving it a nuzzle. If it is the wrong mother it gets knocked away until eventually it finds the right one.

Another benefit of this outlook is that it removes the need for blame, be it of parents, schoolteachers or anyone else. It seems to me that our lives are the very thing we are here to work with, our 'prima materia'. When we apportion blame we miss the point of the drama and of the experience.

There is often a worry in some people's minds, that a model connected in any way with pre-ordination or events already existing means that we can all just sit back and do nothing, or stay in bed all day. I do not really find this a valid argument because it is our nature that drives us into action and our natures are not something separate, but are an integral part of the whole picture and a part of our blueprint. Besides, I have yet to meet the person who does stay in bed all day because of this view!

When I am testing my blueprint and feel uncertain of my direction in life, one of the key things I look for is what I call 'pointers', that is, strong indicators as to what is or is not my direction in life. Sometimes I have attempted to go down a particular path and have run into nothing but trouble, aggravation or unhappiness. Eventually I get the message that this is just not my real path. Valuable lessons may have been learned and necessary experiences gained from the detour, for it is often only in moving away from our true life-path that we see where it really lies. Then there are other occasions where the path opens up in front of me and obstacles disappear and there is a strange feeling of 'rightness', almost as if this is one of the things I am here to do.

To return to the question of free will, the way I resolve it is to transcend it and ask the question, "Who am I?" Is there really a separate entity from which all my thoughts, feelings and desires originate? When I look for one I cannot find it. At first glance I appear to be separate. For example, I can decide to lift my arm and I can lift it but where did the idea to do that come from? Like dreams and artistic inspiration it seemed to come from somewhere beyond 'me' as a separate entity. Einstein also observed that there is always another greater will behind our own ability to will free will.

As with Rumi's story of the ants watching the pen writing we tend to stop far short of the original cause. For if there is only One Consciousness then there is only one will, not lots of conflicting wills.

When this is perceived as part of our own experience the consensus view we have of our separate self generating its own actions begins to dissolve and we become aware of our true identity that is without boundary.

So it is necessary to see through the veils of apparent cause and effect and see the one true cause, which lies in the unmanifest world, and not regard our apparent exertions and efforts as the ultimate cause. But it is also a part of the drama that we do mistake the origin of causes at least for some time. Without that there would be no unfolding drama of life and no world.

Returning to the story of the man from Baghdad who dreamed of the great treasure in Cairo and who, after many adventures, returned to find the treasure in his own house in Baghdad, we can see that we are all rather like him. We know we have lost something yet we look for it on the line of passing time. Eventually we exhaust that search and come to the realisation that it does not lie in time at all, but only in the present moment, and that it is always available in the now. So we discover that the treasure was always in our own house all the time. It is the journey of life that eventually provides this realisation.

Once you have had an experience of the interconnectedness of all things, you can never really see the world and life in quite the same way again. Even when you are caught up in your psychology and in the world of contending opposites this realisation is always there in the background.

# CHAPTER 6

# ILLNESS

Illness is a strange thing. One day we are living life to the full, perhaps with a successful career, social and family life, perhaps a life packed with outdoor pursuits and interests, and never a thought that we could become ill, when all the things we have so taken for granted suddenly come to an end. We never expect this any more than we really seriously consider the thought that one day we will die. Yet suddenly, unexpectedly, often without warning an illness can strike or be diagnosed and you enter into a new world - a world that maybe you never knew existed, a world where there are vast numbers of other people you never knew about, who are also ill, who are perhaps confined to a bed, wheelchair, house or hospital, whose experience of the life you had enjoyed up till then is unknown or seriously curtailed. You are no longer able to partake of the world portrayed in television commercials, where life is so full of promise, excitement and expectation. You enter a world of support groups and therapists. When people ask you how you are you can no longer truthfully say, "I'm fine" or "Very well thank you" as everybody else seems to, but rather: "Mustn't grumble" or "Not too bad today thanks" or "Well actually it's not a very good day today."

Illness is something that can bring all our plans and ambitions to a halt and the path we find ourselves on is not at all the one we wanted or envisaged for ourselves. We may become angry at the injustice of it saying, "But why me? What did I do to deserve this?"

Then you are confronted with a great variety of well meaning advisors each of whom recommends his own favourite cure and each with plenty of stories of miraculous recoveries of people with the same condition. If you seem reluctant to try what has been recommended or if you try something and you don't improve, there is the veiled threat "You do want to get better do you?" or "Well what do you expect if you use that type of treatment?"

With illness you often lose the standing you once had, as if it is something you are doing deliberately, for attention, or sympathy or to get your own way, "Do you seriously think I like being like this, that I want this?" you say. It's almost as if there is a strange hangover in our collective psyches from the middle ages and from Nazi Germany that an ill person is in some way lesser, less collected, less intelligent, less spiritual, or as if the illness brings out a primal fear in the observer, and to acknowledge it would be to admit that you too could get it. So after all the initial fuss has died down you are left with your few really trusted friends and family, thinking, "Well just what do I do now?"

So what causes illness and what is its role in life if any? There are many different models of illness and healing, probably more than there are models of reality. I have found it helpful to look at illness from the point of view of the model of four levels: physical, subtle, causal and Divine.

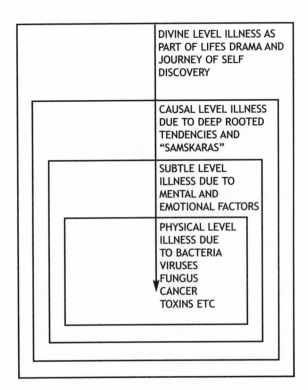

DIVINE LEVEL ILLNESS AS PART OF LIFES DRAMA AND JOURNEY OF SELF DISCOVERY

CAUSAL LEVEL ILLNESS DUE TO DEEP ROOTED TENDENCIES AND "SAMSKARAS"

SUBTLE LEVEL ILLNESS DUE TO MENTAL AND EMOTIONAL FACTORS

PHYSICAL LEVEL ILLNESS DUE TO BACTERIA VIRUSES FUNGUS CANCER TOXINS ETC

**Fig 2. The Four Level Model of the Causality of Illness**

From the physical point of view illness can be seen to be caused by such physical agencies as bacteria, virus, fungus, cancer, toxicity or factors that include genetic predisposition. At this level the disease process can also be influenced by a variety of wider exterior factors such as the availability of treatment in the society in which one lives and the influence of toxins arising from industry and agriculture in that society.

For many this is the end of the story. However, if we enlarge the picture to include the subtle world it can be seen that psychological states affect the physical body and can weaken the immune system leading to a susceptibility to disease. Here again the disease process can be influenced by the wider exterior psychological factors such as how a culture views a particular illness and whether it carries a stigma that influences the attitudes and support of family, friends and health professionals.

This again is not the end of the story. For the subtle world is a manifestation of the causal where the repetition of experiences builds up the possibility of repetitive tendencies, which are then manifest as consequent psychological states and physical symptoms. Thus it is at this deep unmanifest level of the causal body that the seeds and blueprint of illness is stored in unmanifest potential, as is the whole of an individual's life. This might appear to be the ultimate cause of illness but it is still very incomplete, without an understanding of the Divine level.

The Divine level includes all the other levels but also adds important understanding of its own which transforms the understanding of the other levels, giving them an added meaning which they don't have when taken in isolation and not in the context of the whole.

At the Divine level there is no duality, no division into this is good or this is bad, health is good and illness is bad. From the Divine perspective the world and everything in it is seen as part of a perfectly unfolding drama, all unfolding in Consciousness. Illness can now be seen to take on a different role. At the lower level it may still be caused by viruses or bacteria or mental or emotional stress or even deep-seated tendencies manifesting as mental stress and physical symptoms. But these are not the ultimate cause of illness. Viewed from the Divine level, illness becomes a part of the drama of our lives, one of the things we are here to experience so that we can integrate all our varied experiences into an understanding of the One Self or Consciousness of which we are all part. It becomes a part of our life's path or yoga, the thing we are here to work with, part of our journey of discovery and of uncovering who we really are beyond body and psyche.

From the Divine perspective there is no such thing as an accident. You are never at the wrong place at the wrong time, you are always at the right place at the right time. So the physical causes of viruses or toxins are just the physical vehicle for this experience. The emotional and mental factors which may have had their origin in early childhood or other traumatic events are still only the vehicle for this experience in our life's drama, an understanding of which in itself removes the need for any blame at this level. There is no need for the "if onlys"; "If only I'd had different parents, and a different background" or "If only I hadn't caught that person's infection" or "If only I'd been more careful."

From the Divine level there can still be a mystery in causality, but also the ultimate knowledge that it is all for a purpose, a purpose that is probably beyond all rational formulation and understanding. I feel that the mind-body model in isolation often fails in trying to pinpoint the cause of an illness from a rational point of view; this can often lead to a lot of blame and guilt on the part of the person suffering, and is not helpful in the healing process. It is easy to say, "You have this illness because you did that" or "You have this illness because you thought those thoughts, or felt those feelings." From the larger perspective there is still a great mystery in why things happen and I feel that this is very necessary. It may be you develop an illness to prepare you for a future vocation or event in your life, like a deep initiation into the depths of your being that perhaps only an illness can reveal. Or it may be to protect you from something, or to remove you from a situation that is no longer helpful, or to bring one phase of life to a close and prepare you for the next, or even to prepare you for that great letting go, the moment of the death of the physical body.

So we may not understand the full purpose or meaning of an illness but with trust derived from past experience it is enough to know that there is one, and that everything is not only all right but just right. Statistics have shown that people who regard their illness as something to learn from, and as a necessary experience, rather than an inconvenience to be got rid of as soon as possible, often make a fuller recovery.

The writer Thomas Moore suggests that the point of disease is not just to understand the cause and solve the problem but to get close enough to the disease to restore our religious connection with life. We do not cure diseases. Rather they cure us by restoring our religious participation in life.[6]

I am interested in Thomas Moore's concept of diseases curing us by restoring our religious participation in life. I do not think this necessarily means religious in the sense of following a particular religion, but more in the sense of feeling that there is more to life than meets the eye, that we are not just a physical body, that life has a deeper purpose. We have seen how it can be helpful to think of the One Consciousness as having two parts or aspects: an unmanifest Spirit, that underlies the visible world and which is its ultimate cause, and a manifest material creation, which is the expression of that one Spirit. We have seen how it is necessary in our lives to have a balance between these two aspects of Consciousness. When my career goes well, my social life goes well, my health is good, I start to forget the existence of the unmanifest that is experienced in stillness, beyond thought, feeling and perception. And often it is illness that resets the balance. It tells me not to put too much trust in the outer, in ambitions, in material gain. There is something else, something more permanent that I may be overlooking, or not giving enough attention to. It is necessary to let go of the concept of the world as the only reality and in doing this we hit upon a much deeper meaning of illness. We start to see it as an initiation into the nature of who we really are, and who we always have been: the Self that lies beyond body, psychology and potential.

So the process of illness can gradually teach us to transfer our identity of self, from just body or just psychology to that which IS beyond illness and beyond change. We let go of our sole reliance on body or mind as separate entities. It is as if the deep ingrained tendencies or samskaras that separate us from who we really are, are gradually dissolved by illness. This may not happen all at once but by the same process through which they were created, gradually, bit by bit, layer by layer. It is like a piece of cloth being gradually dyed deeper and deeper with each successive dyeing, so that it is hardly perceptible to the eye, yet slowly the change becomes apparent, only in this case maybe the metaphor should be reversed as the cloth is becoming clearer and clearer, and more transparent, as more and more of the brilliancy of who we really are shines through. So illness can be seen as a process of purification, where impurities work their way from the deeper levels of our psyche to be manifest on the surface as physical symptoms, in the same way that a splinter gradually works its way to the surface.

The intensity of illness can make us aware of deep ingrained tendencies or samskaras that might otherwise lie dormant for years, but instead are brought to the surface and dissolved by our awareness of them in the light of the present. From this perspective illness is in no way just an accident with no meaning, or something that just happens when you are not dealing with your emotional issues, or even something that happens when you are on the wrong track in life. But rather it is a part of the process of uncovering and becoming who we really are, a part of our journey of Self discovery; on this journey we are always on the right track, and always learning from experience, for even ignorance, as Bede Griffiths observed, is a stage of knowledge.

In Stephen Levine's book, Healing into Life and Death he relates the story of a lady with cancer, who was berating herself because of her belief that she gave herself the cancer as the "creator of her own reality", and that this belief and the subsequent guilt it engendered was limiting her healing.[7]

It is easy to misunderstand the concept of being the "creator of one's own reality" and its leading to guilt and blame. We may "create our own reality" at one level in the way that we can each see the same event or situation from a different perspective. For one person an event is a disaster while for another person that same event is a great opportunity and a new beginning. Then there is the deeper question of who is the 'I' that "creates its own reality?" Is there just one 'I' that is oneSelf and the Universal Consciousness all at once? The lady in Stephen Levine's story later realised that the idea that she was the creator of her own reality was not so much a falsehood as it was a riddle to discover what that 'I' refers to. The deeper she went the more this 'I' became the whole universe that creates itself out of itself and that maybe she was just taking this statement from too personal a viewpoint.

Stephen Levine defines a large difference between 'cure' and 'healing' in the treatment of illness, in much the same way as Thomas Moore suggests that we don't cure illnesses, they cure us. Often curing the physical condition is not the prime concern but rather allowing the healing at a deeper level to take place. If we allow our sense of separation, of being a separate ego and its opposition to the process of life's unfolding to be dissolved, we let go into who we really are, and perhaps for the first time allow our lives and the lives of those around us to unfold.

In the treatment of illness I would opt for a multi-causal approach where the causes and reasons for illness are as individual and varied as the individual is. This means that the illness needs to be treated at the appropriate level. For example you don't treat blisters on the feet with deep psychotherapy. It's much quicker and more effective and cheaper to get a more comfortable pair of walking boots. The thing I find particularly helpful about the model of four levels is that I am aware that from the fullest Divine perspective, it is still not an accident and it is still about the unfolding of my life's path and about the journey of Self-discovery.

One of the most difficult parts of having an illness is choosing which particular type of healer or therapist to use. I feel that this relates very much to what we saw about the need to identify from which level the illness manifests, as to what would be the most suitable treatment, if indeed any treatment is used at all, and healing is not just left to the body's natural immunity.

In all cases, I think it is very important that the ill person listens primarily to her own inner voice, as to what is the right or wrong treatment for her, and what is the course s/he wishes to follow. It is easy to be influenced by the wishes and stories of others, both of family and friends, and also of therapists themselves. There are however a few factors that definitely make me say 'No' to particular therapists, and see their treatment as limited. One such factor is fundamentalism, in the sense that their particular treatment or discipline is the only true one, and that all others are false, and will just make you worse. I don't believe that in healing any more than I believe it in religion. Our needs are so varied as individuals that we need many different approaches in healing, just as we need many different approaches in religion and philosophy. The next factor is if the therapist claims that s/he can definitely cure your condition, and the third is if fear is in any way involved. This again can be similar to the fear sometimes used in cults to ensure the individual's continued attendance: "If you leave the group you are in the outer darkness and will not have another chance" or "If you leave you will go to Hell". In healing the manipulation used is often of a slightly more subtle nature but the message is basically the same.

So it is important to remember that doctors or therapists do not of themselves heal the person, but rather they are the particular vehicle of Consciousness that is required to bring that particular experience of illness to a close in its right time, once it has fulfilled its purpose in the larger picture of the drama of our lives.

# CHAPTER 7

# LETTING GO

Certain events can chip away at our belief in the world as a separate reality, often from very early on in life, a long illness, the death of a parent or school friend. The experience of bereavement, particularly of a close friend or relative, seems to bring us to the edge of a new world for a time, which makes the events of our day to day lives appear like an unreal dream. It is as if we step behind the curtain of life for a while, and become aware of the unmanifest reality underlying it all. It is not that we come to reject the world and life in the world, but rather it starts to lose its grip as an end in itself. It is as though when we observe life closely it automatically gives us a sense of its own impermanence.

I have a feeling that when we die, it will be similar to waking from a dream at night, and we have an immense feeling of recognition and say; "Of course, this is where I belong, what was that dream I just had?" In the same way we can become totally involved and lost in a film at the cinema and realise afterwards that it was only a film.

In Indian mythology, there are many stories that illustrate this. They usually tell of a man who asks a Yogi or Guru in a clearing in a wood to teach him about Maya or the manifest world of time and change. The Yogi usually brushes the question aside, and soon the man finds himself getting very involved in his life and forgetting all about the Yogi and his question. He marries, has children, builds up a career and gets involved in all sorts of dramas. Eventually his wife leaves him for another man and his life gradually falls apart, and in a state of despair and destitution, quite ready to end his life, he finds himself back in the woodland clearing with the Yogi and his question about Maya still hanging in the air. It is a whole lifetime later, yet no time has passed at all.

Life contains all types of experience and most of us we will have our fair share of the full range of human experience, living in a physical world and inhabiting a physical body, but our bodies must one day decay, our possessions will one day be scattered and our meetings one day will become partings. Such experiences are an unavoidable and inevitable part of human existence.

In this chapter we will look more closely at the role of difficulties, pain and crises in our lives to see if we can learn to see them in a new light and from a wider perspective, and to see if we can learn to look at them, not just as difficulties, but as times of opportunity, change, and possible turning points. In a truly non-dualistic model I feel that there is no event that cannot in some way be turned around and seen in a different light. Just as in some systems of medicine, illness is perceived as failure, so too in some spiritual and philosophical schools, unhappiness is also perceived as failure. Yet it is the nature of life, and part of living in a physical world, that we will experience our share of unhappiness, and our share of difficulties. To deny this or not acknowledge this fact is to deny the nature of life, and to shut off and compartmentalise a large part of our life experience. Yet in order to integrate life all events have to be seen as necessary aspects of a larger whole. It will cause problems if a large part of human experience is branded as something that should not happen. I feel that in order to be transformed and integrated, the experience first has to be brought out into the open and understood or at least acknowledged. It is often when we do this that its true nature becomes apparent, and something we may have tried all our lives to hide from is not at all what it appeared to be when it is looked at without judgement and without preconceived notions of right or wrong, good or bad.

One of the chief causes of difficulty in our lives results from viewing the world and our lives from a limited ego perspective. We do not see the whole pattern of our lives, so we worry, panic or become despondent, when things do not appear to be going in the direction that we think they should. If we really knew for sure that we were being lovingly led through our lives and at each moment being given the best thing possible, then our outlook would be very different, and we would carry on with confidence. How many times have we looked back after a period of great difficulty or uncertainty, and thought, "Why did I get in such a state, it's all turned out fine, will I never learn!" But it is rare that we do know this for certain. Even if we have intimations of it, we do not really believe it, and say, "Well I know it's usually worked out in the past, but this time I just don't see how it can." It is often necessary to keep one foot on the boat and one on the bank, just in case it is all a mechanistic chanceful creation after all, and there is no order or Universal Intelligence guiding it all. Without this definite knowledge, trusting life's process is very difficult, and it can cause me to hang on tightly to what I have. Without the definite knowledge that it is all a part of the process, it is very hard for me to let go. Yet life and growing up is full of such letting go.

Aspects of life that belong to a particular stage of our development may be hung onto beyond their useful time and function. It is as if we go through certain stages of growth, and then at the end of each stage, it is necessary to break out into a wider sphere of being or activity. Just as the endings of stages can be difficult, so too are the birth pangs into new stages of life. It is often a time of great confusion as our ordinary structures and frames of reference may break down and fall away. We may be tempted to retreat into the past, to hang on to old formulations and ways of being, and yet something deep in our nature is inexorably drawing us on.

We try to go back, but the old no longer satisfies, we feel out of place like a stranger, then gradually bit by bit we start to find our new place or path or way of being, it mysteriously opens up before us, not the whole picture, but just gradually one step at a time, and at each step we say "Yes I'm okay" and then we see the next step.

The acceptance of this process is by no means easy, for we are all human beings subject to the normal range of human emotions and fears, and it is natural and right that we become attached to and dependent on certain situations or stages of life. But it is in acknowledging and accepting the difficult nature of life that we can start to change our perception of it. If our objective is just to have all our desires and ambitions fulfilled then our lives will be very difficult, because very often the way life actually turns out will be in opposition to our desires. If we can view our lives primarily as a means of growth and self-discovery, then there will be much less pain, since life then need never be in opposition to our main aim, in fact it is always going our way. This is important, because though our lives may not have changed outwardly, our basic attitude has changed.

One of the great purposes of life, as I understand it, is not to change all unpleasant events into pleasant ones - that would be to deny the very nature of life, which contains all types of experience - but to transform each event inwardly by seeing beyond its surface appearance, beyond the keyhole view, and to really understand the situation from the Divine level or at least to trust it.

Just as it is possible to transform events and experiences

by seeing them from a different perspective, it is possible to look at our emotions and thoughts from a different angle. Part of the journey of discovering who I really am is concerned with self-acceptance, acknowledging and accepting all the different sides and aspects of myself. In order to understand and accept others, it is first necessary to understand and accept oneself, just as in order to love others, we must first be able to love ourselves. Life is a process, and we are all constantly in a state of process, working with the material of our lives, our upbringing, our education and so forth. If we can observe this process in ourselves and accept it, we can also learn to accept it in others. This results in greater understanding and compassion for other people. When we deny this process in ourselves then we will also find it difficult to accept it in others, and it can lead to a feeling of hurt or betrayal, when they do not live up to our expectations. My best way of understanding and accepting the apparently strange behaviour in another person is to acknowledge that I behave in a pretty strange way myself a lot of the time!

So it is important to acknowledge all emotions as being a part of the whole picture of life. Just as a deep sense of happiness or bliss can show us where our path is so too can fear or unhappiness be an indicator of where it is not. Both emotions need to be listened to, and taken notice of. So fear can be seen as an indicator that we are too caught up in our psychology alone, and out of touch with our true Self and its view of reality. Thus that same fear can be used to guide us back to the memory of that Self, and to remember the larger picture. As Stephen Levine says, it then does become one of the stepping stones across the river of forgetfulness.

Because life is a process, when we try to resist its changing flow by holing ourselves up into a cosy corner or hanging on to a past outlived way of life, then life itself has a way of moving us on into fresh realms of experience and learning.

There have been many times when I have seen life as fearful and hostile. When I look closely to see why this is, it is usually because I am being moved forward in my life but a part of me is resisting the change and saying, "No, I still want this to continue" or "I want this to be my avenue in life." Here it is not the events themselves but my perception of them that can vary. The same event can be experienced as difficult or benign depending on my ability to let go when it is time to let go and trust where Consciousness is leading me. In this way events take on different colours depending on whether we view them in a spirit of rejection or as a necessary part of our experience.

I feel also that life and its process of building up and letting go, and the changing stages of life, family, work, relationships, etc, must be a rehearsal for that great letting go, the moment of death. So it is in accepting the impermanent nature of the manifest physical world and working with the inevitable changes and endings in our lives that we prepare ourselves emotionally for the death of the physical body when everything that we have allowed to determine our identity in a worldly sense falls away, and we are left trusting in the unknown.

I've often noticed when I go away travelling that I seem to take myself with me and I come back roughly the same person. I may be in a new country but it still fundamentally evokes in me my usual reactions.

I find it is much more the inner experiences of life such as a major crisis or loss or bereavement that have the power to change me. At times there is the feeling of having passed through a great initiation and I'm no longer the same person I was before the experience. Some deep knowing seems to have been added or maybe it is just that some of the now outlived bits of my psyche have fallen away revealing more of what is already beneath it. It is often difficult to describe in words exactly what the result of this initiation is and yet it is undeniably there.

This is a feeling common to those who have gone through an intensely difficult situation, be it a long isolating illness or similarly stressful event. Your friends and acquaintances may have done lots of interesting things and been to lots of different places, yet you have made an internal journey that is difficult to describe but in no way has it been a waste of time.

The concept of difficulties and troubles in life as an initiation is interesting, though it does seem that it is necessary to bring a certain attitude to bear in order that the experience is felt as a benefit and not just a hindrance. While with some people suffering does seem to result in increased gentleness, openness and compassion, with others it can lead to increased bitterness and anger at the injustice of life.

There is a remarkable story related by George Ritchie in

his book Return from Tomorrow[8] when, as a medical order-
ly during the Second World War, he was in a group assigned
to a recently liberated concentration camp near Wuppertal.
Among the unspeakable horror that they found was a Polish
man whom they called 'Wild Bill Cody' on account of his
drooping handlebar moustache. They assumed that he hadn't
been there for long since his eyes were so bright, his posture
so erect, and he was so full of compassion for his fellow
men, working all hours to help them in his unofficial role as
camp translator and arbitrator of quarrels between different
groups of inmates. Ritchie assumed that he was a recent
arrival at the camp, and was astonished to discover that he
had been there since 1939. Once when Ritchie was telling
him that it was difficult for some of the inmates to forgive
the Germans because they had lost members of their
families, Wild Bill Cody told his own story:

He had lived in the Jewish section of Warsaw with his
wife, two daughters and three little boys. When the Germans
reached his street they lined everyone against a wall and
opened up with machine guns. He begged to be allowed to
die with his family but because he spoke German they put
him in a work group. He had to decide right then whether to
let himself hate the soldiers who had done this. He found it
an easy decision as he was a lawyer and in his practice had
seen all too often what hate could do to people's minds and
bodies. Hate had just killed the six people who mattered
most to him in the world. He decided then that he would
spend the rest of his life, whether it was a few days or many
years, loving every person he came in contact with.

I have often heard it said that the one thing we can always change is our attitude towards a situation or event. We can be overwhelmed by it or use it to our advantage as a learning and growing experience, though I do not quite feel that this is the whole truth. On the one hand the ability to have a good attitude and to take events positively must be to some extent dependent on our natures. For some this is very difficult, if not impossible. Then there are the cases of certain types of illness where the neurological functions are affected, and the part of the mind that can normally effect a change of attitude is no longer effective, or will not work on that occasion. This can be the case in something as simple as the type of depression that can accompany a virus. There is no way out until it passes and no amount of reasoning with oneself will help. I feel that in these and other cases the darkness has to be entered into and allowed and experienced as exactly what it is, darkness, and then seen as an integral part of our experience of life as it is. We may run from this darkness and try to block it out or deny its very existence, for it is very unpleasant and not at all acceptable in a culture where the emphasis is on being successful and healthy and happy. Again it is a question of looking at darkness with a greater breadth and more imagination. In the Chinese book of changes, the I Ching, darkness is used as a metaphor, as the place where seeds germinate, somewhere dark and fertile away from the sun and light. I think that is often very much how it is with us. It is necessary for the psyche sometimes to go into a dark place to be alone, for often it is a time of unseen germination, of deep change, like a chrysalis state of metamorphosis. Life automatically provides this process. We are sometimes in a period of expansion when our direction is outward, but at other times life causes us to contract, to go inwards, perhaps to be alone. In the West great emphasis is put on the need to climb, be it up a material or spiritual ladder, and falling down or sinking can be seen as failure but are we at any time really any nearer or further away from who we really are?

A part of letting go and sinking is the need to come to a state of 'not knowing'. It means letting go of our preconceived notions that I am so and so, and I know this and believe that, letting go of the rigidity of thought that my way is the best way and my views are the best views. Fundamentalism on the other hand is about fixing the mind and hence the heart in an unmoveable pattern. Letting go is about suspending our belief systems so that we can be open to the views of others and really hear what other people are saying and not just how it fits in with our own views. So in this context 'not knowing' is the recognition that we do not have all the answers - if any at all - and allowing our thought to remain fluid and open, not fixed and rigid.

Then there is the letting go of the need to control our lives or the lives of those around us, and being sensitive to the unfolding of each moment, not knowing what our future holds, but being open in each moment to its possibility.

There is also that deep aspect of letting go and sinking and letting be, where we go beyond the rational mind and beyond the thought processes and enter a world of stillness without expectation or experience. It is from sinking into this world of emptiness that a much larger presence can be felt.

It is as if we come here to first build up and then let go, to first try to know and then try to not know. It is in this process, which is provided by our lives and all the varied experiences that we have, that we transcend and go beyond our limited circle of an individual self and connect to and realise our already existing oneness with a much larger whole.

# CHAPTER 8

# SURRENDER

There are times when our path in life is straightforward and clear, there are no momentous events on the horizon, and we have a clear picture of our future direction. It may follow a well-worn and well-loved routine that we have followed for some time, or we may be stepping out onto a new path or a new career with all the expectation of discovery ahead of us. Then there are other times when our life's direction is not so clear. It may have come to an unexpected halt, or we may have arrived at one of life's crossroads where we are unclear as to our future direction. Sometimes it is as if we come up against traffic lights that are red and remain so for some time and we are unable to proceed until they turn green. At other times our well-worn path suddenly peters out and we are left not knowing which direction to take, which career, which relationships, which house to live in, which path to follow, if any path at all. We wonder what to do, who or what to ask. It is a time when we need help or advice. We may be very vulnerable and open to any suggestions, from friends, acquaintances or professionals. We may turn to forms of divination in order to get a small glimpse of how we proceed, or what course of action to take. The main thing is that while in the past we may have been very sure of our direction and path, now we are not, but from whom can we get guidance? Who can really help? From experience I have discovered that there's only one thing I can really trust, for however helpful other people's advice can be and however much they may have helped in the past, the only thing I can ultimately fall back on is mySelf, and I do not mean self in a small sense, but Self in the biggest and fullest sense; who I really am, the part of me that alone knows what is right for me, and that alone knows where my path is leading.

So how do we get that guidance? How do we connect with that Self at moments of need? I think the first thing is the recognition that we are in need of help, that with just our own separate limited abilities we are unable to solve or understand what is before us and what it is that we should do. In this recognition of our own limitations we are already becoming open to the possibility of help.

One of the ways that I have found to be effective in asking for guidance from my real Self, is to ask for a dream to give clarification. I am amazed at how often this method has proved effective. Though it always seems to be very much on a "need to know basis" I only have the dream if it is relevant to the unfolding of that particular path, not as a matter of course. My method is to address the question mentally to my Self several times before going to sleep, something like: "If it is your will, could I have a dream to give me guidance as to what to do in such and such a situation," often the dream comes in a slightly symbolic form, and often it comes unasked for, either as a warning or as encouragement depending on the circumstance. In other instances I have dreamt a particular significant event from the future course of that path, as if I'm being put in the picture as to what proceeding down it will involve, not that I've felt there was ever any choice in the matter, but it prepares me.

There is another much more interesting example of seeing my way when I was having to take a particular course of action, that I felt had to be taken. It was quite difficult due to substantial opposition, so I asked the question before going to sleep, "Do I have to do this? I'm quite happy not to, and I do not want to waste everybody's time, as I'm sure someone else could do it much better, but if I do have to do it, could you let me know?" I repeated this several times before going to sleep for a whole week but nothing happened. Then, at the end of the week, I bumped into a friend who said: "I've had this dream that you are doing something. I must give you complete support, for I do not know what you're doing, nor do I want to know, but I just have to tell you that." I was very pleased with this, for if I had had the dream myself it could have been a case of self-suggestion; the fact that the dream I asked for came through someone else gave it added validity, and also added confirmation to my conviction that at the deeper levels of our being there is no separation between people.

As with any method involving images or words, whether it comes from inside of us or from outside in the form of a clairvoyant or anybody else, it still cannot be fully trusted. The very fact that it still belongs to the world of words and images makes it unreliable. The only truly reliable method is to go beyond the psyche altogether into the stillness of our own Self, which alone knows what is right for us. At the subtle level any impulse is still subject to distortion by our own or other people's belief systems, experience and way of viewing the world. When we become still, we very often have a deep inner knowing and confidence of what is the right thing to do, or right way to proceed, which emerges out of the experience of stillness. It may be that the way to proceed at that time is to do nothing and allow events to unfold without interference. At other times it is necessary to be making an effort even if we are not sure if it is the thing we are meant to do next, because then very often a new direction opens up for us from a totally unexpected quarter that we could never have anticipated, almost as if in response to our effort in another direction.

I am sometimes asked by people facing a crossroads what I think will happen to them or what will be the outcome. While I can look at all the possible choices and make appropriate suggestions, it is often the unforeseen and unexpected option, what I call the 'X factor', that actually occurs. It is some unplanned and unanticipated intervention or occurrence that makes the final outcome totally different from those options at first suggested.

The important thing is to be open to this unknown intervention, because it can happen at the most unexpected moment, usually when we are not planning or even wanting it. The great thing is to be open and allowing, and not so fixedly set on one proposed path or direction that we do not recognise it.

When I am at a crossroads in life or I am worried, fearful or uncertain about an outcome of a course of action, something that helps enormously is the concept of trust. I remember a mentor telling me many years ago, when I was a teenager, about the importance of trusting the Universal Consciousness and acknowledging that. So often since then, when I have been in a difficult situation, the thought has emerged from somewhere deep within me, "just trust the Universal" and somehow the situation always seems to sort itself out. It's also a great thing to do when you wake up in the early hours of the morning, when things can often look big and frightening, again to remember to trust. It feels like resting in the Universal and acknowledging that on your own you cannot see a way through and can do nothing, then often you will be flooded with a feeling of warmth and reassurance as you remember, or it is remembered for you, that it is all right and you are being lovingly carried. The very word remember means to 'put back together', not that we were ever truly separate, but in our mind it sometimes appears so. It seems to be one of the side effects of difficult times that often the only direction to which we can turn is to allow the mind to rest in the present moment, not following any lines of thought that take it out of this state of the silent impartial Witness, viewing our lives without comment or involvement, as we might view a film on the television or at the cinema, while responding to the needs of each moment as they arise.

As we saw earlier, life provides 'pointers' as to our direction. These can come from outside in the form of encouragement for a course of action or chance meetings that give us confirmation or it can take the form of a strong impulse from within to embark on a particular path. Regardless of whether the indicator is internal or external it is still the One Consciousness manifesting through all these different forms.

As we live our lives, there are times when life is outwardly full and everything is building up. We may feel we are on the crest of a wave as years of work come to fruition and our relationships flourish. Then there are other times when everything seems to be falling away - one thing after another. Perhaps a relationship does not work out, or a job comes to an end, an illness develops, or a loved one dies, or sometimes it all happens at once. I'm sure we all know of people where at times one crisis follows another and we think, "Surely they can't have any more?" Yet it is the very completeness of the letting-go process that makes it feel like the workings of Providence. It is as if all props are knocked away until we are brought to the point where we don't know what to do, we are taken to the edge of our experience, and that is the point of surrender. It feels like one of life's strangest and yet most complete initiations. It is a state where all the normal parameters that define our existence in an ordinary sense have fallen away and we are left with a total 'not knowing' though for many of us it is this experience of not knowing and despair that is the great turning point of our lives. It is the point at which we truly see the limitations of our own individual powers and the need to connect with and acknowledge a larger Reality.

The experience of being taken to the edge of our selves is common in great feats of endurance such as mountaineering, polar exploration and other difficult physical exploits. It is even one of the reasons why such feats are attempted. They can have the effect of causing the moving mind to become quiet and we find ourselves in a state of alert presence. Yet life can also provide this same experience. In an extremely difficult life situation, such as an illness, we may be repeatedly taken to the edge of our endurance, where we have no choice but to let go into the experience. It can seem as if all the things that normally separate us from who we really are fall away, our sense of separateness can gradually be dissolved, the normal borders of our existence no longer so rigidly set. We may be forced beyond them to discover physical and emotional reserves we never knew we had, and open up to depths of our selves beyond our normal parameters.

Often as a result of past experiences and upbringing we put imaginary boundaries around ourselves, barriers that we will not go beyond either physically or psychologically, where our sphere of activity has been held in and limited to a smaller circumference by fear or some mental construct of who we are, and what we like and what we do.

It is in coming to this point of ultimate letting go in our life's path that the only option left is to surrender to something much larger than oneself. It is as if at that point we give our lives over to the Universal Consciousness and say, "Thy Will be done." It happens when we are continually confounded in our life's plan. We have tried to make things go our way and make sense of what happens to us and it is at that point of letting go and handing over, that strangely we are led along a new path that was never foreseen, that comes out of the letting go of our ego's need to control our lives. We find that the only option left is to hand over to the Divine and cease to get in the way of the Divine's prompting and direction. It is then like a process where we learn to get our small 'I' and its opinions out of the way. This concept of total surrender, the certainty that whatever happens to me is the will of the One Consciousness, is very difficult for the rational intellect to accept for it's not a question of a myriad separate wills and egos determining the outcome of one's life, but just the one will manifesting in all these different forms and through all these different agencies.

This experience of being brought to the point of surrender often comes as the result of a major life crises, very often in the mid life period. Perhaps up till then our lives have been more oriented to the outward material aspects of career, position and family, but now it is as if we are given the opportunity for a re-orientation for the next phase of life, as if our own Self is calling us to a deeper purpose that is some way more to do with the development of the sacred in life.

True surrendering can be difficult because it is easy to hang on to our own ideas of how we think things should work out, or the direction in which our lives, or the lives of our loved ones, should go. So it seems that surrendering is about having the sort of trust in the Divine and the process of life that admits not one iota of doubt, and this is the natural outcome of recognising the world and all creation as the manifestation of the One Consciousness. If our recognition is only partial, then it is very difficult to truly surrender and know that all is well and that if we let go and fall, we will be caught. If we don't fully trust, what can we surrender to? We will always be worried that what we have surrendered to is just the result of an accident and not the Divine at all.

However, handing over our lives to what the Divine Will wants does not mean abandoning all reason, for it is still necessary to use our power of discrimination, or as Rumi put it "Trust in God but tie the leg of your camel." This means taking guidance in stillness from our own Self as to a course of action but then dedicating that course of action to the Universal and giving up the need to control or manipulate the outcome. It means doing the necessary action demanded by the situation and then giving up the result. As the Tao Te Ching suggests, the only path to serenity is to do your work and then step back.

The process of surrender is not something that we have to go out looking for. I find that life provides everything that is needed at just the right time and even our opposition to the process is not an unwanted accident messing up the drama, but a part of our learning and discovery and a necessary part of its unfolding. Though it is a realisation that we cannot learn just through the intellect, we each have to see it and experience it for ourselves, then this certainty is held by the heart and cannot be lost, and we know that all things are cared for.

Thus it is in relinquishing our control over our lives and allowing in Divine guidance that we prevent ourselves from standing in our own light and allow our lives to unfold, not perhaps in a predictable but far more interesting way than we could have imagined. There are many accounts told by people who had experienced great hardship and frustration in their lives until they were brought to this point of surrender. Then it was almost as if some greater power took over and their lives were filled with synchronistic events that led them along a path they had never anticipated.

The concept of surrender does, I feel, give us another different way of viewing our lives and transforming events, and always seeing the direction of our lives as being to our advantage. If someone asked me, "What is the greatest purpose of our lives?" I think I would answer, "It is to learn to surrender our own separate will to the one Divine Will" and therefore anything that brings us to that point can be regarded as a bonus and not a disaster. It is giving us the chance to reach the highest human potential.

The way of surrender, accepting the Will of God in everything that comes, is not an exclusive way for just a few people. It is a most profound and direct way that dissolves our ego's sense of separation and opens us up to our identity with the One Mind. It is available to everybody in whatever walk of life, circumstance or religion. It can be practised by the mother raising a family, by the commuter on his way to work, by the ill person lying in bed or the child in school. It does not require a change of circumstances. Our own circumstances in which we find ourselves are just the right ones for what we need to learn and know for that moment. The only thing needing to be changed is our attitude to those circumstances. We are no longer working or resting or eating or walking just for ourselves or just to achieve a specific aim, but as a way of serving or acknowledging the One Consciousness. Thus the outcome is not as important as the activity itself. This way we do what is before us to the very best of our ability. We remain in the present and act as the occasion demands, then the outcome is taken care of and can be surrendered. It is dedicated and given over to the Universal.

# CHAPTER 9

# HAPPINESS

O ne of the main motivating forces in human life, if not the main motivating force, is the pursuit of happiness. So much of life and its driving force is guided and initiated by this one pursuit but the way we try to find it differs so much from individual to individual. We look for it in possessions, in relationships, in job satisfaction, in activities, in status, in our looks, in sexual activity, in longer weekends and holidays, in food, in things that we think will block out unhappiness such as excessive consumption of alcohol or narcotics. To some degree all of these things can bring us a certain amount of happiness but is it a lasting happiness or is it in some sense transitory? The possession we thought would bring us happiness after a while no longer does and we want something more. Relationships like our jobs are subject to change, redundancy or possible partings, weekends and holidays all end. I am not suggesting that there is anything wrong in seeking our happiness in these ways. Far from it, for living life to the full and enjoying all the gifts that creation has to offer is so important though I do think that we are limiting ourselves if we view external sources of happiness as ends in themselves. Although we may find it for a while, the changing nature of creation and physical circumstances implies that it will never be permanent. The thing that has been our source of happiness will change or our relationship to it will change.

It is as though life has a cyclic nature, where we go through periods of abundance when it's very full and we are happy, but then the time of abundance ends and we enter a lean and more difficult period, where happiness can no longer be taken for granted. Yet we seek to try to recreate that feeling by trying to go back to the past period of abundance, or looking forward to and anticipating the next one. The nature of life consists of this expanding and contracting motion, in the same way that we have spring, summer, autumn and winter. If it were always summer we would lack the time of contraction, darkness and rest that winter brings, and the rebirth and new beginning that comes with spring. Yet if we are solely dependent on the times of abundance for our happiness, then life is going to be very difficult and will mostly contain unhappiness but with anticipated hope of future happiness, at a time when the circumstances are more agreeable to us.

A happiness that is dependant on external conditions is surely not a real happiness. The great art is in being able to experience it in all phases of life so that happiness is an internal condition and not subject to external events where we are buffeted about like a leaf in the wind.

I have noticed that some people do seem to have naturally 'happy natures' that their basic state is happiness. It's true they do sometimes lose it when a very difficult and traumatic event happens, but then later, once the event has been assimilated, this basic underlying happiness seems to re-establish itself.

With others, they seem to be basically unhappy and though a very good event in their lives can lead to temporary happiness, it is almost certain that after this initial phase, the unhappy nature seems to re-establish itself suggesting that happiness is not so much to do with the events in a person's life but his basic attitude to them.

I have often heard it related that people were very happy while working to build up their careers or lives, but that once they had achieved their goal, or made their fortune, that former happiness seemed to elude them. The happiness was much more connected with the process rather than with the result. I have always observed the same thing in my own life. In the different stages of my career it is the challenge and the building up and the creating that have always been the happiest times. Even with the executing of an individual design or painting, the process of its creation is the thing that brings happiness, once it is complete I go a bit flat and feel a bit lost, until I have started the next one, and then the process begins again.

I have often noticed that much of life's basic happiness comes not so much from the major events, which can bring both happiness and also its opposite, but from the repetition of small things. If I have had a major life trauma and am picking myself up and thinking "I will never be happy again" my advice to myself, and others in the same situation, is do not aim for something really big to bring happiness. Just concentrate on the repetition of small things that each, in its own way, brings a degree of happiness, such as visiting friends whom perhaps one has not seen for a while or going for a walk to a place one loves, re-reading an uplifting book or working in the garden, or whatever it is that we enjoy doing in a small way. Gradually by repetition, from being in quite an unhappy state we find that life starts to become quite acceptable almost without noticing it, and then the bigger events just seem to unfold in their own time when we least expect them.

We still come up against the question of how much we should do to change things in our external world if we are unhappy, and how much we should accept. It is often in acceptance of a situation that unhappiness turns into happiness though first it is important to identify the cause of the unhappiness. It is easy to make the mistake of projecting it onto the wrong thing and thinking "If I had a different partner, job or house, I would be happy" whereas the actual cause of the discontent lies in quite another direction and when that is rectified we actually discover that we really love our partner, job or house and wonder why we could ever have thought otherwise. I have experienced this several times myself. When discontented I feel that if I could change everything it would be all right whereas the real cause lies within. I once stopped a friend selling her house that she really loved, thinking it would solve the discontent she felt which actually lay in a sense of lack in a completely different area.

It is easy to think I would be happy if such and such happened, or if I had a new partner, or if I won the lottery, but I think that this in many cases is just illusion. There is a temporary happiness that comes with the achievement of our goal, but then we revert to our natural state, which is basically how we are now. True happiness is not a result of externals, but a result of internals and in projecting our achievement of happiness onto a possible future life situation we miss out on the 'now' which is probably the only place where true happiness can be found.

There is a traditional fable that illustrates this point. It tells of a magician who could bring about whatever people wished for. One day he visited a village where quite a lot of discontented people lived. One man's wife had left him and he wanted the magician to bring her back. He said, "Yes I can do that but you won't like it" to which the man answered, "Rubbish if she came back everything would be all right". Another man had very little money and he asked the magician if he could get him lots of money. The magician replied that he could "but you won't like it" to which the man replied, "Rubbish, if I had lots of money I'd be perfectly happy." Then there was a couple who had no children and they asked the magician if he could grant them children to which he replied, "Certainly, but you won't like it" to which the couple replied, "Nonsense, if we had children our lives would be complete and we would be happy."

Quite a while later the magician again passed through that particular village. The man who was left by his wife was now back with her but he was unhappy because she nagged him and bossed him around from morning till night, and he said to the magician, "If only you would take her away, for my life is terrible now, much worse than before when it was quite tolerable." The man with little money now had masses, far more than he needed in fact, but he said to the magician, "If only you would take all this money away. I no longer know who my real friends are, people are always trying to borrow or steal from me, and now I'm so unhappy whereas before life was quite tolerable." The couple with no children now had lots of children but they were terribly badly behaved and caused chaos all around the surrounding countryside and were constantly in trouble with the police and one even burnt their house down. They said to the magician, "If only you would take all these children away, for life was quite tolerable before."

The moral of the story is that the circumstance you find yourself in at each moment is the one that is just right for what you are here to learn and experience, and it is in the acceptance of our circumstances that we find contentment.

So we return to the question of how much we should accept our lot and find contentment in things as they are, and how much we should strive to change our circumstances if we are unhappy? Only a madman would accept a bad situation if there were genuinely a way out. In the same way only a mad person would remain ill if there were a certain cure on offer. So finding happiness via the route of acceptance is only appropriate when it really is impossible to change the outer circumstances of life that are giving rise to the feeling of discontent on that occasion. If not, it is like the story of the man who was drowning and prayed to God to rescue him. After a while a lifeboat came along but the man said, "No it's all right, God will save me". A while later a helicopter came along to rescue him but the man said, "It's all right, God will save me." Later, after he had drowned, he appeared before God and said, "Why didn't you answer my prayer, after I asked you to help me?" and God replied: "I did, first I sent a lifeboat, then I sent a helicopter."

Although this is a light-hearted metaphorical tale it does illustrate the fact that Consciousness is constantly manifesting itself to us in forms that we do not recognise.

Once you do realise that it is impossible to change a particular situation, then at that point acceptance becomes much easier, though it may be a question of the paradox, the ability to live with two opposing views at the same time, that is very important. For one of the keys to happiness is to be able to be accepting of one's condition or state, at the same time as striving for a different one, and to feel no conflict in this. Then it is possible to make the decision to be happy with life just as it is, to choose joy, and I think this is what the story of the people who all wanted something different is really about. You can always be wanting your life to be different and have the unhappiness that is caused by your ego being in opposition to how things are, "But I wanted this to happen", or you can simply make the switch and change your point of view, learning to "want what you have", while simultaneously allowing life to unfold and being open to the possibilities latent in each moment. I have noticed that if I do panic and try to control my life or try to manipulate events it never works out.

Much of our difficulty in life arises because our heart becomes set on a person or a direction in life that is simply not on our 'blueprint' or life script. It is on our blueprint to the extent that to continue pursuing it becomes a learning experience and eventually we learn this fact and the nature of life's unfolding. So it is a question of being open to each situation, but not being manipulative or hanging on when a situation refuses to unfold in the way we want it to. For it is impossible to miss something that is a part of our life's script. When a particular event or person does have a part to play in our future, apparently insurmountable obstacles will fall away in a way we never could have anticipated and we will be provided with what it is we need at that particular time. If persistence, determination and patience is required for that situation, then that is also provided within our natures.

Gently allowing our lives to unfold and being open to the unexpected has a very different feel from being driven by our limited ego and what it thinks it wants. It is a process that reminds me of a fish in a river facing the current and remaining in place by just a slight flick of its tail. We appear to be 'doing' everything and yet at the same time we are in reality 'doing' nothing.

The psychiatrist and Auschwitz survivor Viktor Frankl[9] points out that if we pursue happiness or success for itself it usually eludes us, for it comes as a by-product of following a feeling of rightness in oneself, of dedicating oneself to a greater cause or calling without consideration to the material outcome. So by not looking for it and not pursuing it, happiness, or whatever it is we truly want at a deep level, unexpectedly finds us.

I was in the Australian outback on an expedition to look for dinosaur bones.

While crossing one very long and desolate plain, we saw a funnel of wind, dust and bits of scrub, moving ominously back and forth by the road. It was what the Aborigines call a 'willy-willy', a small tornado.

While I was out exploring the surrounding bush, early in the afternoon on a hot still day, I suddenly heard a roaring sound, like an express train, coming towards me through the trees. Suddenly through the trees in front of me emerged a powerful 'willy-willy'. It was like a great spinning vortex of hot air and dust and bits of tree branch. It was powerfully drawing in the still air from all around it, and violently shaking any gum trees it hit. At first I ran from it. But then I was drawn back to it, as if it was like a strange magical living being, from the Aborigines dreamtime. I had a desire to be right at its centre. It departed as quickly as it had come, off through the trees and across the river and the afternoon was still again.

Several times I saw more 'willy-willies', but they were always in the distance, and I so wanted to be at the centre of one, I would drive after it but it would elude me. Then one day right at the end of the expedition, I was on a large stony plain, engrossed in the pieces of fossilised wood that littered the area, and that told of a time in Australia's remote past when the plain was forest. I heard a rushing sound behind me. I turned, and suddenly I was being whirled at the centre of a 'willy-willy'. It found me.

Another aspect of happiness is the concept of contrast. There is not really an objective measure or standard of what should make us happy, but rather we are often happy by contrast to what we are used to. If the thing or situation that makes us happy becomes too available or too habitual, eventually it loses its ability to generate the same happiness it once did. As in the saying, "He is richest whose pleasures are the cheapest" by taking things too much for granted we no longer appreciate them or no longer see them. If we have experienced a particularly difficult time or a time of great unhappiness or physical limitation, a brief cessation of that situation can lead to an intense happiness from what would appear to the observer to be a perfectly ordinary or even quite an unpleasant situation. Thus it is not always easy to judge a person's state of happiness from their external surroundings and life situation, regardless of whether these appear good or bad.

Again Viktor Frankl gives an example from his experience at Auschwitz[9]. Sometime after the war someone showed him a photograph of prisoners lying crowded on their bunks and said how terrible this was. Viktor Frankl was genuinely puzzled by this as he remembered how they longed to be indoors and resting and not out on the torturing grind of the work party from dawn till dusk when beatings and death could come at anytime. So for him it was a photo of people who were probably not so unhappy.

The same is so after years of illness where maybe the ability to walk or run or just move has been lost. When it returns, even if only briefly, there is sheer delight in something that we normally don't think about at all and just take for granted. This can be another unexpected benefit of illness, that through it we are able to regain our sense of wonder at something we had taken for granted. I remember hearing a talk by a lady who had been blind since birth but who, later in life, had an operation to give her sight for the first time and she just could not believe what she was seeing when she looked about her and saw such things as trees. She could not understand how all the rest of us were not permanently in a state of awe, because we could see this wonder all the time. Yet our perception of the miraculous that is all around us flags, because we stop looking and cease really seeing due to our over familiarity, and then we need to seek for something that is in some way overtly sensational or miraculous, forgetting that everything that surrounds us all the time is miraculous. This same process can happen when we know that our death is very near and we are perhaps seeing our surroundings in that form for the last time. We start to really see in a way that perhaps we had not done since early childhood.

There are moments in life when we have this vivid memory of an object or a view, when we see it as if for the first time. It can happen with quite ordinary day to day objects, perhaps sitting at the breakfast table, when suddenly we see as if directly and our perception is not obscured by thought or preconception. It usually happens when our mind is for some reason suddenly stilled, for the still mind can find delight and happiness in all things.

I have one memory that is still very vivid, when I was painting in the Isles of Scilly. It was a bright sunny morning at the end of September. I set up my easel and laid out my paints on the sun-dappled needles under a group of pine trees overlooking the sea. The part of my mind that normally gives a running commentary seemed quieter. It didn't want to question and comment on everything and as a result all the landscape around me seemed much more vivid. It just seemed to sparkle and had a strange innocence and freshness about it as if I was seeing more than just the surface projection.

There was another occasion when I was quite young. I was staying on my uncle's farm in Cambridgeshire one Christmas. It has been snowing quite heavily and I went for a walk across the fields. Dusk was just beginning to fall and there was a slight pinkish tinge to the sky. I came into a valley that contained some old thatched barns. They were just standing there timelessly in the snow and gathering dusk. It was a moment full of emotion and mystery with hints of something deeper that I cannot quite described. I can still see that scene and myself watching it, so clearly now.

There is another very important aspect to happiness which emerges from a still mind and which we touched upon in the chapter "Who Am I?". This is the unconditional happiness that suddenly emerges from within, often regardless of circumstance, that is one of the properties or our true Selves. Then all our other experiences of happiness are just seen as a reflection of this one Great Happiness. We may appear to experience happiness in people, places and events, but what we are really seeing is the one true Self reflected in all these various forms, and yet these manifest forms are also stepping stones to this reality. Each one can hint at and remind us of its existence. We may suddenly experience intense happiness when we hear a piece of music, or see a well composed picture or building, or a beautiful view, or animal or a person we like, all hinting at the Reality of which they are the reflection.

When we desire things in life, whether it is objects, situations or people, the very act of desire takes us out of the present moment awareness and the satisfaction with this moment now as it is. With the fulfilment of our objective, the desire ceases and we return to a feeling of contentment with the present moment. This leads us to believe that happiness came from the object we desired when in reality it was due to a temporary return to a state of no desire. The cause of the happiness was in us and not in the object. After a while we may want something else and the cycle starts again. The remedy for this situation is the realisation that whatever is before us is the manifestation of Consciousness. Whatever is before us is "It" in all its fullness. As this attitude gradually permeates our being, so too does a deep inner happiness that is not dependent on passing time but is the nature of who we really are.

It is very reassuring that one of the properties of our true Self is this unconditional happiness that is not dependent upon circumstances, and that this source is always available to us whatever our condition in life. However bad things may sometimes appear on the surface, at any time and often when we least expect it, it can become apparent, and we receive glimpses of a realm of transcendence. So again it is not a question of creating anything new, but simply a recognition and acknowledgement of that which already is, and is ever present as the ground of our being.

Seeking to be happy is sometimes seen as a selfish pursuit, although there is really nothing selfish about it, for when we are happy ourselves we are in a much better position to help others, and much more able to play our part in life. Also happiness seems to radiate outwards to those around. Though in the paradoxical manner described in Viktor Frankl's experience of how happiness is not something to aim at but rather something that ensues, it is often when we take the attention off our small selves and do things for others or for a cause greater than ourselves that we find happiness quite unexpectedly.

There is one further important aspect to being light hearted and that is humour, particularly as manifest in the ability not to take oneself too seriously. When we see the humorous side to the world, to ourselves and to the different situations we find ourselves in, already we have disengaged and are no longer so caught up by the world of appearances. To find ourselves funny is very healthy, if not it is possible to become very earnest and dogmatic in the "my way is the only way" mode, with a need to dominate and control others. The people I have really trusted as my mentors in life have always, as well as exuding a deep inner happiness and kindness, also had the sparkle of humour in their eyes.

The experience of this Great Happiness; the happiness that comes from an intimation of our own true Selves is so powerful and so all embracing, that everything else seems to pale beside it. The petty events and dramas of our lives that once seemed so important no longer do so. It may be that we only experience the smallest split second of the sort of stillness that allows this happiness to manifest, yet because the deeper levels of our being are not subject to the limitations of time and space that we associate with the physical level, the smallest experience of this sort of happiness can have an effect on our lives and on our surroundings that can transform a day, a year or a lifetime.

# CHAPTER 10

# TURNING THINGS AROUND

The model of reality that we have been looking at is one in which almost every event or situation in life can be turned around and seen from a different perspective. Often this may be from a completely opposite viewpoint from our normal one, as if when we look at the world we are seeing it reflected in a mirror, and that what we see is a back to front version of how it is in reality.

We saw how we normally perceive the manifest physical world and universe as the primary reality with mind and Consciousness as remote specks deep in our brain, and yet the reality is probably that it is the other way around, with Consciousness as the primary reality, and matter as a ripple or manifest expression of that Consciousness.

So from this view Consciousness is not something far away and remote, but immanent right now, in every aspect of life that we encounter, and the only thing that really needs changing is our perception; the only thing that really needs doing to see it the right way around is to acknowledge everything as the One Consciousness. At first our attempts to remember to acknowledge everything as the One Consciousness are only partial and spasmodic, but gradually as a result of repetition in all sorts of different circumstances, it starts to become a part of our nature to look at the world in this way, though it is important to remember to suspend the day to day analytical mind which will always want to know the causes and purpose of events. That need to know has to be replaced with trust - trust that there is a purpose on a level beyond what our rational mind can grasp.

When we look at our lives we normally judge the events in them from the context of a life of three score years and ten. When we use the phrase, 'expect the worst', we refer to the death of the physical body and indeed most of our worst case scenarios involve death. But supposing, looking at it from the right way round, death is actually the best experience of our lives, a return to who we really are, and where we really belong, a return home? Such is the case of a near death experience related by Dr Raymond Moody[10] where a medical student resuscitated one of his professors after a cardiac arrest. The professor's first words to him were, "Never do that again". Later he explained to the student the reason for his angry words, that "he had brought him back to death not life." Does not this change of attitude to a broader perspective regarding our life span give us a very different view of many of the events in life that we find incomprehensible and that make us sometimes ask the question, "if there is a God, how could he allow bad things to happen?"

There is a story found in India, in the legends of Krishna, that illustrates how things are not always what they appear to be on the surface. It tells of how Krishna and Arjuna, while travelling together, stay at the house of a very rich man who treats them very badly. In the morning Krishna blesses him by saying that his fortune will increase even more. The next night they stay at the house of a very poor man whose only possession is a cow. He treats them very kindly but the next morning Krishna blesses him by saying that his cow will die. Arjuna is very puzzled by this behaviour and asks Krishna to explain the meaning of his actions. "The rich man", Krishna replied, "was very attached to his wealth and by giving him more wealth I was doing him a disfavour by adding to his attachments. The poor man, however, only had one attachment standing between himself and liberation and that was his cow so by taking his cow away I was really blessing him."

There is another story, very similar to this, in the Jewish scripture, The Talmud. Instead of Krishna and Arjuna it features Elijah and Rabbi Joachanan.

These two stories are very remarkable and significant. They hint at a very different way of viewing the world and events for how often are we not unlike Rabbi Jochanan or

Arjuna and exclaim in dumb amazement at what we perceive happening around us or to us and the apparent injustice of it, lacking this deeper knowledge beyond what we are able to perceive with just our five senses? This is not in any way suggesting that we should not act to alleviate suffering or combat injustice. Naturally we try to eradicate suffering within the sphere of our capabilities and wherever possible we listen to our own inner sense of what is the right thing to do and what is the wrong thing. When we are unable to change or affect a situation, then it has to be turned around and seen in a different light.

The story of Krishna and the poor man's cow is, I feel, particularly significant in relation to how we understand and judge apparent ill fortune such as illness or other experiences of loss. Of all the different models and explanations this is the one I always return to, as it does not contain the blame and judgement element that can so easily belong to those models advocating solely physical or psychological causality such as, "If you hadn't done that action you wouldn't be in this position" or "What did you do to attract this event to yourself?" From this other view, however, the unfortunate event can be turned right around and can be seen as a blessing. How do we know that it is not the fire that is required to burn away that last little bit of impediment that obscures who we really are? As Viktor Frankl said, "What is to give light must endure burning."

Thus from this view illness and loss are not necessarily an unfortunate curse, nor the sufferer a lesser human being, but rather they can be regarded as a privilege, like being put on a special course of yoga, or on the fast track at an airport to bypass the normal long queue. Rumi, writing in the Mathnawi, uses a metaphor to express this view when he talks of the chickpea boiling in a pot and how it keeps rising to the top of the pot full of complaint as to its lot in life. The cook hits the chickpeas with a ladle and says: "Boil nicely, I am not hitting you because I detest you, but so you may get taste and flavour and mingle with the Spirit".

The Russian writer Alexander Solzhenitsyn[11], who spent many years as a prisoner in the Russian labour camp system under Stalin's oppressive regime, came to a similar conclusion. He felt that the only way he could understand the suffering that he and other inmates were put through was to understand that the meaning of earthly life lay not in prospering, as we usually think, but in the development of the soul. From that point of view suffering is inflicted on those whose development holds out hope. He was prepared to bless the prison for having been a part of his life.

Here Solzhenitsyn expresses this fundamental change of perspective, the necessity to change our viewpoint right around, to move beyond duality with its judgements of good and bad fortune, blame and punishment. He touches on one of the fundamental changes of attitude required; it is not that the meaning of life depends on prospering, but on the development of the soul, in discovering the profound mystery of who we really are beyond the constraints with which we limit ourselves within the field of time. This insight can emerge out of the most extreme and testing situation and is often a pre-requisite for it.

When life is quite pleasant and I am not put under pressure, then I am quite content to move along the line of passing time and become caught up with its demands and its drama. It often requires something fairly momentous for me to see beyond the surface reality of day-to-day life, to disengage from it and reconnect with my real depths and heights and enter the ocean of happiness that lies beyond passing time with its experiences of pleasure and pain.

The other key tenet that Solzhenitsyn touches upon is his view that difficulties in life are given to "those whose development holds out hope". So that the experience of suffering is neither a punishment nor a misfortune brought on by oneself, but a means of transcendence that is given to be used, to enable us to transcend our normal limitations, precisely because we possess the capacity to do so. This is a reversal of the view of suffering being deserved in a negative sense, because we have done wrong, but rather of its being deserved in the positive sense, that we are ready for the transcendence that its experience will allow. It does shed some more light on the mystery touched on in the story of Krishna and Arjuna as to why the fates that people suffer do not, on the surface at least, always seem to accord with our views of justice or causality. There is a traditional Chinese fable that illustrates the need to reverse our ordinary way of thinking and of viewing events. It tells of how a poor farmer had a horse that ran off into the country of the barbarians. All his neighbours offered their condolences but the farmer said, "How do you know that this isn't good fortune?" A few months later the horse returned bringing with it a barbarian's horse of excellent stock. All his neighbours offered their congratulations but the farmer said, "How do you know that this isn't a disaster?" The two horses bred and soon the farmer had a whole herd of fine horses. One day when the farmer's son was riding one of them he fell off and broke his hipbone. All the neighbours offered the farmer their condolences but he said, "How do you know that this isn't good fortune?" A year later the barbarians invaded the frontier and all the fit young men were called up and most of them died in the war but the farmer's son survived. Thus good fortune can be disaster and vice-versa. Who can tell how events will be transformed?

So we can learn to turn around the view we have of almost all the events in our lives. One of the first stages in seeing a situation from a new angle is learning to no longer resist it, to transcend our limited ego perspective in favour of that of our true Selves. When we are in opposition to a situation, we have already closed ourselves to the possibilities that are inherent within it. So it is first necessary to suspend our usual judgements and look at the situation and what is being offered. If there genuinely is no way out and no alternative, then it has to be turned around and seen in a different light.

In order to bring about this change of view, it is important to remember that our lives are unfolding according to a precise script or plan and that we are in no way the victim of accident or unfortunate circumstances, but rather that this is a time of opportunity, perhaps given to discover some talent that we didn't know we possessed, or to discover or uncover a part of ourselves that we were unaware of. One of the ways in which I make such times harder for myself, is that when I get into a new and unwelcome situation I tend to think of it as lasting forever, rather than being finite and limited in time, and only for a definite period or until its function or purpose is complete.

I can think of several examples from my own life where a particular situation has been forced upon me through no apparent choice of my own, but then, by turning the situation around to my advantage, it has turned out to be a blessing and something has been achieved that otherwise could not have been possible.

There are two occasions when my design work has completely dried up due to both recession and changes in fashion. On the first occasion I was able to devote my time to landscape painting and the further refinement of my drawing technique. On the second occasion I turned to writing and the assimilation of my life experiences. On both occasions my design work re-emerged in its own time once I had the necessary rest.

There are other times, perhaps due to illness or the end of relationships, when we find ourselves alone and without our usual support systems. In accepting the situation, I find it important to be able to turn 'loneliness' into 'aloneness' or 'solitude'. Rather than feeling like a misfortune it can be seen as an opportunity for deep introspection and recuperation, a chance to go deeper into ourselves and discover aspects of our natures that otherwise we would just skim over. I sometimes think of it as a time for being like a

Himalayan Yogi in a mountain cave, but again its duration always turns out to be finite and then I think: "I should have made more use of that opportunity."

There are so many ways that the events we regard as misfortunes can be turned around to become blessings. Redundancy and loss may in a strange way allow us to connect with those who should be close to us, or those less fortunate than ourselves, from whom material success or excessive activity may have cut us off.

The death of a loved one can be a reminder to reconnect in a deeper way with those people close to us that we still can reconnect with and to let them know that they really are loved ones.

When we experience grief at the loss of a friend or loved one we grieve also for all our past sorrows when perhaps we were, for some reason, unable to grieve properly or fully. At such times we also, whether knowingly or not, grieve for the separation from our own true home and true origin. The wave-like motion of grief can melt our sense of separateness and wear down our hard boundaries, opening us up into a much larger sphere of being, and a deeper connection with others. It emerges at unexpected times, when we have become too caught up with the superficial aspects of life, reminding us to remember our depths, and to rekindle a longing to return to and become who we really are.

I have also noticed that the more I am in touch with my own still centre, the closer I feel to those I love regardless of whether the separation is caused by death or just physical space. I feel this is because at the deepest level of our being there is no separation between ourselves and anybody else so at this level we are never separate from those we love.

Another one of the aspects of life that can be turned around is our understanding of time and the way that we perceive it as an objective concept flowing from the past into the future. We have already seen how the experience of illness for example can prepare us for an event or vocation yet to come, thus suggesting that its causes are actually not in the past but in the future. This portrays an image of time not necessarily flowing in one direction, but more like a stream with whirlpools, eddies and back currents where past and future exist in an eternal present.

There are certain times when memories and feelings that are long forgotten are suddenly brought to the surface of our consciousness, as if we are reliving them, or they had just occurred recently, as if it is allowing a deeper understanding and integration of this earlier time. Perhaps at the time we were unable to give the situation our full attention and had to put our thoughts and feelings to one side in order to cope with the practical demands of the moment, and its reliving allows it to come into the light of the present and be healed.

There can be a mysterious inner connection between events in our lives that is nothing to do with the ordinary sequence of time. An event or time in our lives can connect for no discernible reason with an earlier time.

When we look at time from the perspective of the four levels we can see that our experience of it differs according to the cognition of those levels, as time is dependant upon matter, when we move away from matter our concept and experience of time changes. For instance in the subtle world of our dreams time is very different, an apparently very long dream can take place in a very short amount of physical time, whereas in dreamless sleep there is no concept of time. The moment of falling asleep to the moment of waking can appear like no time at all, and yet often many hours have elapsed. Also in our ordinary daytime waking state our concept of time can vary greatly, For instance, when we are really enjoying ourselves time can appear to move quickly and we may want it to slow down and go more slowly while at other times, when we are not having quite so much fun, it seems to drag and we look at our watches again and again to see hardly any time has passed. It is often reported that time is different again in experiences of expanded states of consciousness, perhaps because we move away from the solely physical to an identity with the deeper levels within us. This often happens in moments of emergency when time can slow right down and events appear to take place in slow motion.

There is an example from my life when I was about eleven. It was a stormy, windy day and I was out with a friend walking along a riverbank near my home. We came across a long row of very tall poplar trees that grew along the edge of the river. One of them had blown over in the wind and I started climbing along its trunk as it lay there in the water meadow. I remember hearing my friend call out and looking round I saw that a second tree that had stood adjacent to the one I was climbing on was falling towards me and had already reached 45 degrees. At that point time seemed to go into slow motion, there was no panic or fear, I knew that I had to fall off my tree and this I did, again in slow motion, as I heard a mighty crashing sound all around me. When I hit the ground time returned to normal and I ran out of the trees very shaken. Looking back I saw that the second tree now lay full length along the trunk of the first tree where I had been standing, having split the latter's trunk. It had been a very close call with death.

In the meditative state it is possible to enter into the causal realm of no time and no experience, although rather than being done unconsciously as in deep sleep, it is entered into consciously as we transcend the thought processes and enter a world of stillness, though as with deep sleep there is no experience at this level, we only know later by its effects that we have been there. Because it is outside of our normal experience of physical time, its effects and influence can be out of all proportion to its duration. When we identify ourselves with our thoughts we are connected with movement and time, and are subject to the changes, judgements and dualities of that world, but when we stand back and become the Witness we enter into the timeless moment 'Now', and it is that same Witness that is always there, timeless and unchanging, through all the different phases of our life.

Thus the main aspect to turning things around is that touched on at the start of this chapter, the discovery and realisation of our own true Selves and the necessity not to see Consciousness as a remote spark waiting to be uncovered after years and years of intensive work and struggle but rather as something here now. When we perceive something as far away and remote, then for us it is, and when we only acknowledge its presence in those aspects of life that we understand or that appeal to us, then it will remain elusive and remote, a glimmer here and a glimmer there, something that belongs to a time in the future, when we are in a better state and in better circumstances, and the world is arranged in a way that appeals to us. In striving to experience Consciousness at some future time we miss the fact that it's here already, and that it is manifesting in its appropriate form in this moment now, both internally and externally in whatever we experience.

In seeking a 'miraculous' experience, we miss the miraculous nature of the present moment as it is, because we want things to be different from what they already are.

This underlines the paradox of how we may set out to seek Consciousness, which is probably necessary, but in the end we come to the realisation that there is in reality nowhere else to seek it, and no real obstacle to its perception, other than our inability to see what is already there. This is in keeping with the principle of not aiming too directly at the thing we are seeking but rather letting it find us. If we try too hard to find something we miss it, as in the story of the fish who swam off to search for this stuff called water.

# CHAPTER 11

# ABOUT LOVE

In the west today we generally have one word for the phenomenon known as Love which is confusing since it is used to describe a very diverse and often contrary range of feelings. In some cultures the need for a greater differentiation of meaning was better understood and several words were used in place of our one word. In the Indian Hindu tradition the word prem is used for the experience of Divine Love, bhakti as the way to the realisation of God through love and devotion, and kama for the passionate erotic love between the sexes. In Greek the world agape was used for the experience of spiritual love, or universal compassion, and eros for sexual desire. Later with the troubadours of the middle ages came the concept of falling in love or romantic love, being led by your heart and what it tells you, for which the Latin word amor was used.

It often remains a great mystery as to why we are suddenly attracted to a particular person, sometimes in spite of our more rational judgement, and often across the conventional barriers of age or nationality. It can manifest as a strong initial attraction upon first meeting someone, or an attraction that grows gradually as a result of acquaintance, and getting to know all the different sides and facets of someone. Sometimes we are attracted to people out of need: needing to belong, needing to be loved, needing to love, fear of being alone. Sometimes our attraction is due to projection. We project our own images of what we want onto the other person, and do not see them as they really are. Or we are hurt when they do not live up to our ideas of who we think they ought to be.

I am amazed at how often I have been attracted to people from whom I have had to learn a particular lesson, or who are acting as mirrors and showing me some truth within myself. Their role in my life is often just for the duration of that lesson or experience. While some relationships are of longer duration, others are like stepping stones and it is important to be able to recognise this and let go once their purpose has been fulfilled.

As we have seen there are so many meanings to the word 'love'. It can be the attraction between the sexes, which includes romantic love and sexual desire, or the deep affection we may feel for our children, parents, family and friends or a more general mystical experience of love when our affection is not limited to particular people or objects but is directed outwards to all creation.

But what of the sensation of 'love', what are its hallmarks? I think that one important hallmark is an alteration in the boundaries that normally define our sense of self. M. Scott-Peck[12] in his book The Road Less Travelled describes how when we fall in love our normal ego-boundaries that define our sense of self are dissolved and we have a feeling of expansiveness and intense happiness and a connection with a wider circumference of being. For a time we are in a quite different state in relation to ourselves and the world around. Any feelings we may have of loneliness and fear evaporate, the world loses much of its hostility. But regardless of who it is we may have fallen for, this initial period of intense emotion always passes, and our ego boundaries return to their original position. Yet this initial attraction plays an important role, for it can be the stepping stone to the experience of a deeper and more lasting form of love. It is first necessary to make the decision to commit ourselves to this process of attending to another person, and for that the period of intense emotion that we call: 'falling in love' is often necessary. Yet when those initial strong feelings die down the chance for a deeper, more realistic love begins. This comes out of a committed decision to show love and affection, even if at times it is not always felt emotionally. When the ego boundaries are stretched in these circumstances they do not always return to their original circumference so that genuine growth and expansion is achieved.

I feel that this same process can be observed in those relationships that we have not chosen in quite the same way as in romantic love. Close family relations can feel more like 'given relationships' where there can be a deep love and affection but at the same time a need for independence and space, in which to grow onto and follow our individual life paths. It is in allowing and working with the different prejudices and varied limitations that we all possess, and in learning to show love and affection in these circumstances, rather than just walking away, that our ego boundaries are also stretched and to some degree permanently dissolved. It is in this voluntary stretching of ourselves for another, or for a cause greater than ourselves, that our sense of separateness can gradually be dissolved, and we can feel a connection with a much greater whole, which is a large part of the experience of love.

The mystical concept of love is not dissimilar to the feeling of being in love with another person. Rather than this intense feeling being directed towards just one individual there is no single object to which it is directed. It is as if there is an internal ocean of love and an external ocean of love, and as our separate ego starts to dissolve, there is a free flow between these two inner and outer worlds, forming a single ocean, which is how it must be in reality. In this process we just become a transparent vehicle for love.

Again I find it helpful to turn to the model of four levels as a framework for looking at the concept of love and attraction and seeing it in a different light. At the physical level of attraction I see someone's physical form, the shape of their body, the colour of their hair, the shape of their face, their eyes, their smile, their voice, and I am attracted to them. It is all in accord with what I regard as attractive. I don't always quite know why this is, any more than I really know why the composition of a particular painting appeals to me, or the work of a particular artist, for it is often a very subjective experience, and it varies from individual to individual. What for one person is the most beautiful being they have ever set eyes on, is for another, someone of no special interest or beauty and visa-versa. This is a very fortunate arrangement, as otherwise we would all fall in love with the same person. Also at this level is the purely physical aspect of sexual attraction and desire, the biological urge to reproduce, what Joseph Campbell calls the zeal of the organs for each other[3]. When I ponder on why I find someone's physical form very appealing, I think it is often because the physical body is a manifestation of the subtle or psychological body. What is in our subtle bodies is clearly manifest in our physical forms, in the way we hold ourselves, in our faces and expression and in our eyes and voices. Just from our features we can show qualities such as pride, kindness, hardness, fear and rigidity.

The subtle world is the realm of both emotional and mental attraction. After I have been physically attracted to someone I start to talk to them, and I may be attracted to their way of thinking, to how they express themselves, whether they have a sense of humour or not, what their outlook on life is like, whether we have things in common. All this is a part of attraction at the subtle level, and as it is also the realm of individual experience, it is the level at which we experience emotion, and the level at which we experience greater or lesser degrees of separation from those around us.

We saw earlier how what we experience at the subtle level is a manifestation of what is contained in potential at the causal level. While we can for a time put on an act at the level of our psychology, eventually what is contained at this deeper level of our nature becomes manifest. Often when we first meet someone we are on our very best behaviour and are able to put on a show of being the kindest, sweetest person, totally without faults, whoever existed.

People may wonder, "Is there nothing wrong with this person at all?" and we may say, "Yes I'd love to do the washing up" and "Yes I'd love to go to the opera", even if it is the thing we least like in the world. Gradually, as we drop our guard and stop trying so hard to impress, aspects of what we are really like at this deeper level start to become manifest. For instance I may have a strong temper, that for a while I am able to conceal, but eventually little by little it becomes manifest, until I make no attempt at all to conceal it. It is just as possible for another person to bring out our unmanifest and unsuspected talents that lie dormant at the causal level, that may contribute in a major way to our unfolding and flowering in life. Another person's influence often enables us to set out on a new path in life or start a new vocation that before was totally undreamed of.

There is another aspect to love and attraction at the causal level, and that is the unaccountable connections we sometimes feel for people, as if it is far more than being physically attracted or a meeting of minds, as if we already at some deep level know or have known this person.

There are many explanations given for this sense of recognition and knowing that we experience with some people. Some explain it in terms of past lives or reincarnation. For myself reincarnation remains an idea since I have no reliable direct personal experience of it, though I suspect that it is a metaphor for a reality that is infinitely more subtle than anything we can formulate or explain with our rational minds. Is not our real Self outside the cycle of birth and death? So reincarnation, if it exists, applies to a very limited part of a whole being, a part whose apparent separation we perpetuate by mistakenly identifying Self with just body or psychology. My own suggested explanation, that I touched upon in an earlier chapter, would be that we recognise people or events, or have intimations of their approach, because at the level of our deepest Selves we already know the entire script of our lives, and at times we experience echoes of this memory. It is not surprising that we experience this sense of knowing when we first meet someone who is to play a significant part in our lives, or we have an intimation of the approach of an important event.

It is also significant that the people who we learn the most about ourselves from, are not always the ones who we have the most harmonious relationships with, so this deep level of connection can take many forms and is not necessarily about falling in love in the conventional sense.

Beyond the causal is the Divine level perspective of love

and attraction. The Divine level is the abode of our true Selves and at this level there is no individuality and no separation. The concept of ego boundaries applies only to our experience at the subtle level. At the Divine level there are no boundaries, yet our experience of it in its pure form is limited, due to the fluctuating nature of our psyches and our mistaken identity of Self with just body or psyche. The Divine level is sometimes described in mystical literature as an "ocean of unconditional love" or as the Beloved and all the longing for love that we experience is but a distant memory and reflection of this realm of universal love.

So remembering that the Divine level is not a remote realm deep in our beings but the broadest possible understanding of all the levels, we can start to understand the various manifestations of love from a new and deeper perspective. We are attracted to someone not just because they appeal to us physically, nor just because they appeal to us mentally, nor just because we may have a deep causal attraction, but ultimately because these are aspects of and reflections of the One Universal Love. So what we are seeing is our own true Self reflected in the other person, and the part of ourselves that is capable of love is that same Self. So that ultimately it is the Self that sees and recognises itSelf. In looking at someone's physical form, we may just see a body of flesh and bones, or we see the manifestation and reflection of the beloved. Thus in seeking the experience of love and its dissolution of our normal ego boundaries, we are also seeking the ocean of love that has no boundaries.

It is in recognising that human love in all forms is a

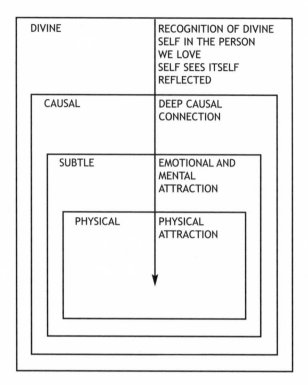

**Fig 3. Love and the Model of Four Levels**

reflection of the Great Love that it becomes another route back to the transcendent ocean. Love is not something we have or feel, but something we enter into. And not something we have to create, but something already existing that we uncover and become aware of in deep stillness. So the experience of this ocean is dependent on us being who we truly are and on dissolving our misconceived notions of separation and duality.

There are many different aspects of life that contribute to the melting of our finite sense of self, and allow us to open more fully to the experience of love. One of these is compassion. It is a word derived from the Latin, the literal meaning of which is; 'with-suffering', that is the entering into and sharing of another's sorrow or pain. After we have been through an intense period of suffering it is very difficult to see someone else going through that same experience without wanting in some way to help or support that person. Suffering is shared because we know what it is like, and even if we cannot alleviate it in any way, we are able to empathise (Greek; 'in-feeling') and support emotionally if not physically, not in a spirit of condescension, but out of mutual respect for what the other person is experiencing.

For compassion is the practical result of the realisation that at the deepest level we are all one, that what I do to another I do to myself, hence the injunction in the Gospels, "Do unto others as you would be done by".

I have a small practical example of this from my own life. When I was sixteen I learnt a method of meditation that I have practised ever since. I was at school at the time and up until then I had perceived the teachers to be people to be fought against but soon after learning to meditate my perspective changed and I saw them as people who were just trying to earn their livings and probably didn't want to be teachers at all. I found that I suddenly wanted to help them and make life easier for them instead of trying to obstruct them.

There appear to be two movements in creation: the out flowing form from the One Undivided Consciousness into all the multifarious forms of creation, from One to many. Then there is the return to the Source, the movement from the many to One. When we practise methods such as meditation we use our discriminative mind to gradually move our identification of self back through the causal chain from matter to spirit, from transitory to eternal. Compassion is the result of the descent from One to many. It is the practical realisation that all the varied forms we experience are the manifestation of this One Consciousness, and that all are equally deserving of love and mercy. Having disengaged our identity with the purely temporal and found our true identity, we then discover that all the things we have disengaged from are also a part of that true identity, not as external separate objects, but as all parts of one whole. So in compassion the boundary between ourselves and another becomes weaker or dissolved. I remember after someone I loved very much had died, whenever I saw a person being separated from someone they loved, even if only for a while, I would find myself overcome with emotion. Before my experience of loss a similar situation would not have had the same effect on me. So my loss softened the usually well-defined boundaries to my sense of self. I believe that this is one of the ways in which the mystery of love is a part of the mystery of suffering. The drama of creation, with its limitations of time and space, birth and death, meetings and partings, in a strange way allows love and compassion to unfold. The fact that a physical creation must inevitably include pain, suffering and loss is the very thing that brings out the possibility of love and compassion. If it were the sort of creation envisaged by those philosophies advocating a literal physical heaven on earth, where there is no suffering and no pain, then this opening up of the individual to the Universal in compassion, and the expanding of limited boundaries to limitless, would be impossible.

It is often when our limitations are broken down, even if temporarily, and our concern for the needs of the passing moment suspended, that quite unexpectedly we open ourselves to love.

# CHAPTER 12

# FREEDOM AND LIBERATION

Like happiness, the pursuit of freedom is another key issue in human life and is the chief motivating factor in many different human endeavours and pursuits, from philosophies, religions and political movements, through to wars and revolutions. Yet what does freedom really mean and what are its implications for the individual?

I find that we can gain an insight into the concept of freedom by turning again to the model of four levels. At the physical level we are subject to the limitations imposed upon us by virtue of having a physical body that exists in time and space and is subject to birth and death, growth and decay. It normally requires warmth, shelter and food in order to survive and all this has to be obtained by our own efforts. There are further limitations imposed upon our physical bodies by factors such as our health, our mobility, our wealth, the type of political system under which we live, and the physical circumstances into which we are born. At this level we appear to have a degree of free will, we appear to be able to make efforts to better our physical conditions, to strive for a better job or career, and in the end arrive at a lifestyle that has fewer limitations and hence more freedom. However, even at this level there are many possible limitations to our freedom that are totally beyond our control or sphere of influence. For instance, we may lose our health and hence our mobility. We may live under a totalitarian regime that imposes great limitations on our personal freedom, and on the way in which we think and express ourselves.

How and what we think and feel cannot be forced and regulated by external laws since the subtle world, the world of psychology, is our own private domain which no one else can see. Here too true freedom is often limited. What we think and feel is to a great extent conditioned by our upbringing, background and experience, factors that in themselves give rise to set patterns of behaviour that are reflected in the way we act and respond to situations on the physical level. Our attitudes can often reflect a particular generation or sub group of society to which we belong and we may be quite unaware of this at a conscious level. In this way we may describe someone's behaviour by saying, "Well of course they belong to the wartime generation", or

"They're a Sixties person". We are also subject to the limitations of the changing moods and desires of our own psyches and their power to pull us first in one direction and then in another, often against our better judgement.

Thus at the subtle level we are often bound by our habits and ways of reacting. This can be observed in the way that situations in life have a tendency to repeat themselves in various forms as if a message is being gently amplified until we are able to hear it.

Again at the subtle level we may feel we have free will, that we are the masters of our own destinies, that we can decide whether or not to embark on a particular course of action. Even when we do find that we are limited by our own emotional and mental habits that are leading us into repetitive situations, can we not attempt to modify our behaviour in much the same way that we may feel that our physical bodies are in need of modification in the form of a new hairstyle or diet? Since what is at the subtle level is a manifestation of what is stored in potential at the causal level, working at the subtle level alone may prove ineffective if the causes of a particular type of behaviour remain intact in the same way that trying to remove weeds from our gardens by simply cutting the weed down and leaving the roots only gives temporary relief.

Is our behaviour, our will and our potential for true freedom not determined by our blueprint, that is laid down at the causal level? Is it to this level that we must address any modification if we are to make the changes that lead to freedom, both from limiting circumstances and from a limited sense of self? But how do we know what these modifications are? Is it really effective for one aspect of our psychology to look at and judge another aspect when we may not understand the role it may be playing in the whole unfolding drama of our lives? When a particular aspect of our nature has played its necessary role does it then not gradually start to fall away of its own accord?

I feel that the answers to these and other questions and to the whole concept of freedom, can be found not by taking the physical, subtle and causal worlds in isolation, nor by any amount of modification to these levels alone, but rather by looking to and remembering the existence of the Divine level. This is the abode of our true Selves, which is both beyond and yet also includes the worlds of body, psyche and potential. It is in learning to listen to the impulses and guidance coming from this Self, and in aligning our separate ego with this One Will, that we can find freedom.

It is as if the pattern for our lives is already totally in existence at this level, and if we are able to trust in it, then it can unfold in a way that is beyond the capacity of our rational minds to comprehend. Part of this unfolding includes the gradual transcending of our sense of separation and the process of coming to our Selves and finding our true path in life. When this happens we are no longer in opposition to the process of life's unfolding. We create trouble for ourselves when we forget the existence of our true Selves and perceive ourselves as separate individuals with separate wills who can make the world go whichever way we want. We experience pain when, despite our best efforts, events just will not go the way we think they should. This process, however, is not a mistake or an individual messing up the Divine plan. That is quite impossible. It is more a question of the way in which we learn from experience, so that we gradually come to our Selves and realise that the One will is also our will by reflection.

When we are in tune with the process of life's unfolding, no matter what our particular circumstance may be, there is a feeling of great harmony and freedom within each moment and of not being in opposition to life's process. That is not to imply that at one level we may not be working to change our circumstances or recover from an illness or even fight great battles, if that is what the unfolding demands, but simultaneously, at each moment, there is also the total acceptance that this present moment is perfect, just as it should be, and contains no opposite. Later our ego mind may reassert itself and start wanting to re-write the script, but here again we can use the experience of the pain that being in opposition generates, to guide us back to our true Selves and our life's path.

It is a great paradox that we really are already free, we already are the Self. Yet due to habit and past conditioning we usually experience ourselves as separate, limited and bound. So our work of coming to ourSelves consists in turning around and seeing through these illusions that our psyches create, and learning to perceive the world and our Self as it already is.

This is not always quite as simple and straightforward as it may at first sound as it requires turning around some very deeply ingrained habits and attitudes, and it contains the pitfall that we may end up just strengthening our limited ego-selves in the guise of spiritual development. True spiritual practice, in my experience, rarely makes any claims for itself, nor do those involved in it see themselves in any way better or superior to others, or themselves in a more privileged position. Rather they are aware that everyone is being led towards that same realisation, each in their own individual way and that the same Self is equally present in all beings.

This is relevant, since I feel that we are no longer in an era where very dominant and charismatic leaders are important. This need for a strong external figure to lead us can often be a projection brought about by an inability to connect with and recognise our own leader within, or our own source of knowledge that is ever present and available to us all the time.

When we learn an art, be it painting, music or any other activity or vocation requiring great skill, it usually takes years of practice to learn the basic rudiments of the technique before we become proficient and able to acquire a degree of mastery, out of which a certain freedom of expression can then develop. I often see this process in the work of great painters who, having mastered the techniques of painting and drawing, can then gradually start to simplify their work until eventually great meaning can be expressed with just a few economical strokes of the brush. In the same way an athlete, sportsman or dancer can give the impression of effortless simplicity only because of the years of persistent and unrelenting practice that have gone before. Imitators often try to go directly to this state of simplicity yet without the mastery of technique required, and the results are often rather embarrassing and without the depth of feeling conveyed by those who have followed the full path. I think that this same process applies in the pursuit of freedom generally. It is a state arrived at by a particular process and not just by a letting go of all the normal constraints and limitations that we may feel confine and restrict us. We have seen that even when the normal physical constraints to behaviour are removed, there are much deeper limitations still imposed upon us from deep within our own natures. A change of physical circumstance does not alter this, any more than a change in political philosophy alters the basic nature of mankind, as various social experiments in new types of government testify.

It can seem strange that while our true Selves are complete at every moment and in need of no modification, at the level of the drama of life we have to pass through a series of developmental stages. It is important that these stages are not bypassed in any way, nor that spirituality is used as a means of avoidance rather than integration.

It is very easy for an interest in the spiritual to become a retreat into the past, and away from the responsibilities of adult life. Or it can be used as a way of avoiding looking at certain issues within ourselves that may need attending to. Perhaps they are areas we have shied away from as a result of deep hurt, or we may have missed out on a particular stage of our development that is demanding attention. Rather than addressing it we elevate our dysfunction into a spiritual virtue as a means of avoidance.

In the world's mystical and religious traditions ultimate freedom is the liberation from the small illusory self that is bound by mind identification to the line of time, and awakening to our true identity that is always free from the limitations of time and change.

This can be seen in a small way when, during a time of trauma, we may wake up in the morning and for a few seconds there is just stillness and Being. Then the mind becomes active and reminds us of what we have to face or what has happened and the stillness is lost.

The root word budh in Sanskrit may be translated as meaning "to regain consciousness after a swoon". Thus a Buddha is one who has awakened to his true identity. It is a lovely feeling of release like waking up from a bad dream or coming back to one's true home. Thus it is said that no one actually becomes a Buddha, you simply cease to be deluded. The ninth-century Chinese Zen master Huang Po[13] emphasised that there is nowhere we have to go to find this realisation. Rather, whatever is in front of us is it. If we begin to reason about it we miss it. This suggests that each of our lives just as it is expresses the Universal. This can seem at odds with those traditions that employ a series of steps towards realisation. But perhaps this is just a metaphorical way of gently helping our minds to give up their sole identification with form and acknowledging what is.

There is a further aspect to the question of freedom when we look at the idea of karma, a concept found in both

Buddhist and Hindu doctrine. It suggests that due to the law of cause and effect, we are constantly reaping the effects of past causes, and constantly sowing the seeds of future effects. It is an idea usually associated with the doctrine of reincarnation, so that seeds sown in one lifetime are said to bear their fruit in the next. It does raise an interesting point, namely, that working at this level alone real freedom is impossible since we will always be bound by the effects of past causes. If we have created negative karma, then we must return to reap those effects, and if we have created positive karma, then we must also return to reap those effects. Even if it means a life of pleasure it is still not liberation.

In my understanding, karma is not a form of punishment or retribution brought upon oneself by previous actions, nor is it even the reaped results of past causes, but rather it is the process of experience by which we are gradually made aware of the existence of our true Selves and the true nature of Reality. As Joseph Campbell[3] points out, in different traditions different metaphors are used to illustrate this point. In some eastern religions the concept of reincarnation is used, while in Christianity the idea of purgatory has been used. Yet both concepts are metaphors for the fact that we may need something more in the way of experience to remove our ignorance of the underlying Reality.

Certain concepts are used in the spiritual traditions for the purposes of training, and some of these are dualistic concepts that later have to be discarded once the Reality is perceived at first hand, in the same way that we may use a thorn to remove a thorn and then discard both. I believe that this is the nature of the more literal understanding of the law of karma. Its existence is dependent on the illusory notions of our being separate independent doers, and of the existence of a separate sense of self, so that when with the eye of true perception Reality is seen, such concepts are seen to have no real existence.

The key to freedom can ultimately be gained only by going beyond the more limited physical, subtle and causal worlds, at which such laws of causality operate, and thus no longer seeing them as separate realities having their own independent existence. Are not these worlds ultimately our own projection and the result of partial or limited perception, when in reality there is only the Divine or Spiritual world? When we identify with these levels within ourselves we perpetuate the illusion of separation and of being a separate doer and creator of our actions. So if karma exists as a universal law of cause and effect, the escape from it cannot just be by creating better causes, or increased merit, or paying off karmic debts. It has to be through realising deep in our being that there never was a separate entity to accumulate karma or debts in the first place and in this way acknowledging the One Consciousness of which we are all part. In playing our own part in life's drama and not wanting this moment to be other than it already is, we see that we already are that which we are seeking.

# CHAPTER 13

# MEANING

It is observable that different people going through the same or similar experiences often react in totally different ways. The same experience may bring out the very best in one person, while for another it becomes a source of bitterness and self pity.

Viktor Frankl observed this process during his time in Auschwitz.[9] Whilst many of the prisoners sank to a level of bestiality not dissimilar to that of their captors, a few were able to rise above it, and use the experience as a means of self transcendence. The reason for this he observed was dependent on an individual's ability to imbue the experience with meaning. The problem with indefinite imprisonment, as with long-term or chronic illness, is that the meaning cannot be based on reaching a definite date of release, or an end to the illness at a particular moment in time.

Rather than the meaning being based on the knowledge or hope of what we will be able to do at a particular time in the future, it has to be derived, not from a retreat into the past, but from the experience itself. In the case of pleasurable or creative activities, it is easy to see how the process can give meaning but in the case of suffering it is often not so easy. As we saw in the chapter on illness, in order to survive and become enriched by the experience, meaning is necessary, and is the one ingredient that we ourselves need to add to any situation in order to transform it into a means of transcendence, for if we apportion blame, either to self or others, then we miss out on this possibility. Although our true Selves are beyond definition and categorisation, at the level of our daily lives meaning is very important.

We have seen how finding and following our life's purpose is an integral part of discovering who we really are. So 'meaning' can come from using all the varied experiences of our lives as a means of transcending our limitations and breaking out beyond our normally limiting sense of self and who we think we are.

So we can give our lives meaning when we see the challenge presented to us by each new situation, and see each situation as a means of transcending and integrating our small ego-based selves, and opening up to, and becoming who we really are. That does not necessarily imply a mighty struggle but simply a fundamental change of attitude to ourselves and the world around. It is in using life as our vehicle for transformation that we give meaning to all our different experiences whether they are of illness, loss, love, relationships, happiness or whatever they are.

I do not believe that the realisation of our true Selves necessarily means that we become a radiant Buddha or saint-like figure living permanently in bliss, something that can be just an egoistic fantasy born out of an inability to see the value of our own lives and what is already around us. For each one of us Self-realisation is a matter of living our lives in a manner that is truly unique to ourselves and ultimately the fulfilment of our purpose in life, and that is something we can only know from moment to moment.

Returning to Viktor Frankl's experience in Auschwitz and our own experience in life, why is it that some people do manage to imbue their lives with meaning and use difficult situations as a means of transcendence whilst others become overwhelmed by the difficulties? Are the former in some way better human beings than the latter? Is it due to genetics, nature or upbringing or is it as a result of something that is beyond the causality of body, psyche and nature? I feel that a verse in the Indian scripture the Mundaka Upanishad contains a clue. It suggests that the true Self is not reached just through the intellect or sacred teaching but rather the true Self is reached by whom He chooses. My understanding of this is that it is the impulse to discover and unite with our own true Self that comes from the true Self. It is as if the Self unfolds itSelf to itSelf and ultimately attains itSelf. There is no question of those who do not manage to find meaning in a situation being in any way less than those who do. Rather it is that it is not yet their particular moment for this unfolding. There is also no question of chance or missed opportunities. It seems inevitable that we are each led along our own path of realisation at just the right time.

All of us are just aspects of the One Consciousness playing different roles in the great drama of life. Just as we often feel compassion for the 'victims' so too can we feel compassion for the 'villains' in life as we imagine what it must be like playing that role.

Once we have this desire to discover and connect with our own true Selves what else can we do? What more is there than the approaches already suggested? My own particular method, in addition to trying to see everything as a part of One Consciousness in my daily life, has been a technique of mantra meditation in order to bring my mind to stillness on a regular daily basis but there are a great variety of different methods and techniques available today to suit people's differing needs. It is important that each person finds the particular approach or method that is suited to his/her nature and uses it in order to experience its full range of possibilities. I think that two of the hallmarks of genuine practice are the experience of both inner stillness and its accompanying sense of unconditional happiness. That is not to say that with the varied nature of our lives we will have this experience all the time but there will be moments when this is so and such moments act as incentive bonuses to reassure us that we are on the right track. They encourage us to go on and persist and not to be disheartened. In addition to this comes a more general feeling of stability, as if we are more deeply grounded in our true Selves and less easily knocked off course by life's events. Sometimes we may think that not much is happening, but little by little our boundaries to self are being dissolved. Often we ourselves are the last people to notice this process because it is so gradual.

There are many other ways in which we open up to ourSelves, anything that takes us beyond our limited egos. It may be a method of meditation, prayer, yoga or dancing. It may be following a religion or philosophy and finding its inner core, that part beneath the surface dogmas that deals with Self-Realisation. It may be in our lives, by really giving ourselves to an art or vocation, or another person, or a cause greater than oneself.

I am continually amazed at the amount of perfectly ordinary people I meet who practice no particular method to my knowledge, who seem to have a radiance and holiness about them such as you see on the faces of great saints. It may be the delivery man at the local shop or a lady confined to a wheelchair and yet just living their lives has become their means of transcendence.

There is an old saying that goes, "Once the disciple is ready the teacher appears." I think that this is a principle that applies to all the different fields of endeavour in our lives; we meet the thing or person or situation we need when we are ready for it, and when we are ready to move on to the next stage in our lives. Our particular means of transcendence will often present itself without our having to go out looking for it; it finds us. It may initially appear in a form in which we can appreciate it but then appear later in a different form as our understanding grows. As with relationships so it is with philosophies. We sometimes need a series of stepping stones until we are ready for what is most suited to us. Indeed, if our concept and understanding of truth does not continually go through a process of change and refinement, and we think we at last have all the answers, then we have merely become stuck in one particular form at one level. While we may well stay on one particular path our understanding of what it is telling us should change and become deeper and fuller as we mature.

There may come a stage when, although we may remain deeply grounded in a tradition, it is necessary for us to come into our own knowledge and no longer just be a mouthpiece for that tradition. We are no longer solely dependent on someone else's revelation from the past, which will always to some extent be conditioned and limited by its manifestation in time and space. At this point we have to open to the knowledge of our own Self in the present in a way that is suitable for us as individuals and for playing our own particular role in life's drama. It is often said that a true teacher is not someone who tells you what you ought to know, but rather someone who shows you how to contact your own source of eternal life within yourself, so that you can answer your own questions.

When we hear something that is true for us, there is a feeling of recognition and we may say "Yes, of course", and that again is because we are not being shown anything new but only reminded of what deep down we know already.

In some traditions there are two stages in the realisation of our true Selves. It reminds me of the concept in chemistry of a super-saturated solution, where we can go on dissolving crystals in a solution until it reaches the point where the addition of only a single crystal causes the whole solution to solidify.

The first stage, our day-to-day efforts to come to ourSelves and acknowledge the all pervasiveness of the One Consciousness in all the different situations we encounter, is like the process of gradually adding crystals to the solution. To the observer the solution appears unchanged but in reality it is going through a steady but gradual transformation.

The second stage is the addition to the solution of the final crystal. In many of the Japanese Zen Buddhist stories it is the intervention by a teacher or master at the appropriate moment that provides the final catalyst for full realisation. The same thing happens on a misty morning when the sun suddenly breaks through and all the mist dissolves.

The same Consciousness that can manifest as a teacher, is also manifesting in all the various forms we encounter, and any of the various forms can be used by that Consciousness as the catalyst. It can be an illness or dark night of the soul experience, or any one of a number of different forms, and it may be that we all have a moment of great opportunity in the death of the physical body, and that this is the very thing our lives are preparing us for so that our lives can have meaning in relation to death. From this point of view the realisation of our true Selves is not a gradual process but rather it is the preparation for it that is gradual and all the events in our lives are a part of this preparation. They are a part of the process of adding crystals to the solution so that none of our experiences in life are wasted. They are all a part of this process of coming to ourSelves.

In recent years, due to technological advances in science, there has been a great increase in the number of people being resuscitated after they have been pronounced clinically dead, and consequently a great increase in the number of accounts of Near Death Experiences. These I feel give us great insight, not only into the nature of a possible life after death, but also into the nature of this opportunity and what is necessary to prepare for it. The most significant part of the experience in the majority of cases recorded is the meeting with a very bright light, which is often described as a Being of light, from which radiates an intense amount of unconditional love. People often describe a feeling of recognition for this light, as if it is someone we know even better than ourselves, or it may be like falling into the arms of a beloved parent, or something we have been searching for all our lives and did not know it.

These experiences are not dissimilar to the after death state described in the Tibetan Book of the Dead[14], where the different deities are experienced in the form of light. The key to liberation is in realising at that moment that this is but the light of our own true Selves, or what in the Tibetan Buddhist tradition is called the 'nature mind' and hence merging with it and recognising that any experiences of doubt or fear are just the projections of our own limited psyches. In mystical literature this merging of the individual with the Universal is often described as a 'wedding'.

In St Matthew's Gospel there is a very interesting parable that can I feel be understood in relation to this experience at the moment of death. It is called the "parable of the wedding garment" and it tells of a king's son who is to be married but when the guests are summoned to the wedding they all make excuses. So instead the king sends his servants out into the highways to gather people so that the wedding is furnished with guests. However, when the king greets the guests there is one man who is not wearing a wedding garment. The king has his servants bind him hand and foot and cast him into the outer darkness. When taken literally this appears as a very enigmatic and unjust parable for the man without a wedding garment did not know that he was going to be invited to a wedding. Yet parables are a metaphorical way of expressing a particular concept and need not be taken too literally. I do not believe that it is really possible to miss an opportunity, but rather that it is simply not yet our moment or time for that particular experience. However, the parable does make an interesting point. It shows that something is needed in the way of preparation for the moment of death, which can come unexpectedly at any moment, in order that this wedding with our true Selves can take place. It is this preparation for death that can be one of the main factors that gives meaning to our lives and makes sense of many of the otherwise incomprehensible episodes.

In order to recognise the Being of light as oneSelf at death, I believe that it is necessary to start well in advance, seeing that same Self in and behind all the different aspects and phases of our lives, no matter how contrary they may sometimes appear to us, till it becomes our second nature to do this, and also to recognise that during our lives when we experience doubt or fear, that it is the projection of our psyches, and to use that experience to guide us back into the present, to our true Being, our own place of no fear that is always available and is beyond birth and death.

It is in acknowledging all sides of life as part of one whole, that we integrate all our experiences into that Self, and all our life becomes the preparation for that ultimate moment of letting go and surrender. Living our lives fully and playing our own part in life's drama, however insignificant it may appear to the whole, is an integral part of that process. Marie de Hennezel, a psychologist working with the terminally ill, observed that it was not faith but the texture of a life lived that allowed one to give oneself into the arms of death.[15]

This emphasises the need for us to have the courage to follow our own inner light and our own path, so that we have no regrets and are able to let go more fully. I sometimes find it helpful to say to myself, "If you knew you were going to die next week is there anything you would regret not having done", and if there is, I try to do it as soon as possible, be it anything unsaid that needs saying to someone I value, right up to starting a new vocation or career, if the one I am currently following is not the one I really wanted to follow, or has outlived its value and usefulness.

Viktor Frankl[9] suggests that there are three main ways in which we can arrive at meaning in our lives. The first is by creating some work or doing something; the second is by experiencing something or someone so that "experience" becomes as valuable as achievement. This opens up the avenue to meaning for those who, due to their circumstances, may be incapable of physical achievement and also gives a balance to the inner and outer worlds of achievement and experience. The third way he suggests, which is open to anybody no matter how difficult their situation in life, is the ability to transform or grow beyond oneself and in so doing turn a personal tragedy into a triumph. All life provides the means for this journey no matter what our particular circumstance or life situation and often the more adverse our circumstances are the greater is the potential for transformation.

It is because the nature of life is one of constant change that we are eventually led to find our true Being in the present. If we remain solely at the level of the drama then life's changing fortunes will just present us with an ever-changing cycle of success or failure, pleasure or pain.

In the same way that our lives gradually evoke our characters, so too our lives can take us back into the greater depths of the different levels of ourselves, if we can learn to look at them from a different point of view and regard them as our means of transformation. So we are gradually taken from the more limited and finite, to the less limited and infinite, from the physical through the subtle and causal to the Divine. The varied events in our lives can be the very things that cause us to realise that we are not just the physical, and later that we are not just the psychological, and that we are not just our deep causal potential, but ultimately we are 'That' which is without boundary and is beyond all and yet includes all.

Thus in trying to comprehend the meaning behind all the varied things we experience and the events we see in life, it is necessary to return to our starting point; that reality can never be fully understood nor fully explained in rational terms, but rather can only be hinted at metaphorically. The reason why it can never be fully understood or explained rationally is because, as we have seen, it is impossible to understand the Divine level with the cognition of the subtle level.

Although the answer can never be rationally explained in a satisfactory way, nevertheless there are times when we may get a glimpse of it, when momentarily we see things from the perspective of the Divine level, and it comes across as a wordless deep inner certainty and inner knowing that all is well, the rationale of which we really don't understand and yet we know deep in our beings that this is so.

I have often heard people talk or hint at secret knowledge, but I think there is no greater knowledge than the realisation that everything is a part of and is, the One Universal Consciousness, any other knowledge just refers to details or methods for realising this one truth. It may be an idea that has at times been disguised or hidden simply because of the fact that it cannot be rationally explained and hence is easily misunderstood. If we observe our lives from this point of view we will see that we are all the time being presented with signs or hints that this is so. What previously appeared to be a veil now becomes a signpost. In discovering that we are being lovingly looked after and carried during our lives and that there are in reality no opposites, that same confidence and certainty in life's unfolding can be carried over into death.

# REFERENCES

1   Andrew Weil, The Natural Mind, Boston, 1972.
2   P.D. Ouspenksy, A New Model of the Universe, p.XVI
    2nd edition, Routledge and Kegan Paul, 1934.
3   Joseph Campbell, The Power of Myth, Doubleday, 1988.
4   Retold from Sir Laurens Van der Post at 80, BBC TV
5   C.G. Jung, Memories, Dreams and Reflections, Fontana,
    1983.
6   Thomas Moore, Care of the Soul, Piatkus, 1992.
7   Stephen Levine, Healing Into Life and Death, Anchor
    Books, 1987.
8   George Ritchie, Return from Tomorrow, Kingsway
    Publications, 1978.
9   Viktor Frankl, Mans Search for Meaning, Washington
    Square Press, 1985.
10  "Into the Light", Retold from BBC Radio 4, 1987.
11  Alexander Solzhenitsyn, The Gulag Archipelago,
    Volume II, Collins and Harvill Press, 1975.
12  M. Scott Peck, The Road Less Travelled, Arrow, 1990.
13  John Blofeld, The Zen Teaching of Huang Po, The
    Buddhist Society, 1968.
14  W.Y. Evans-Wentz, The Tibetan Book of the Dead,
    Oxford University Press, 1957.
15  Marie De Hennezel, Intimate Death, Warner Books,
    1998.

Philip Jacobs can be contacted at: philipjcbs@yahoo.co.uk

# O

is a symbol of the world,
of oneness and unity. O Books
explores the many paths of wholeness
and spiritual understanding which
different traditions have developed down
the ages. It aims to bring this knowledge
in accessible form, to a general readership,
providing practical spirituality to today's seekers.

For the full list of over 200 titles covering:

- CHILDREN'S PRAYER, NOVELTY AND GIFT BOOKS
- CHILDREN'S CHRISTIAN AND SPIRITUALITY
- CHRISTMAS AND EASTER
- RELIGION/PHILOSOPHY
- SCHOOL TITLES
- ANGELS/CHANNELLING
- HEALING/MEDITATION
- SELF-HELP/RELATIONSHIPS
- ASTROLOGY/NUMEROLOGY
- SPIRITUAL ENQUIRY
- CHRISTIANITY, EVANGELICAL
  AND LIBERAL/RADICAL
- CURRENT AFFAIRS
- HISTORY/BIOGRAPHY
- INSPIRATIONAL/DEVOTIONAL
- WORLD RELIGIONS/INTERFAITH
- BIOGRAPHY AND FICTION
- BIBLE AND REFERENCE
- SCIENCE/PSYCHOLOGY

Please visit our website,
**www.O-books.net**

# Everyday Buddha

*A contemporary rendering of the Buddhist classic, The Dhammapada*
Karma Yonten Senge

These quintessential sayings of the Buddha offer a rich tapestry of spiritual teachings and reflections on the spiritual path. More than just a collection of Buddhist sayings, *The Dhammapada's* message is timeless and crosses all cultural boundaries. It offers the reader a constant source of inspiration, reflection and companionship. It is a treasure trove of pure wisdom that has something to offer to everyone.

*Everyday Buddha* brings the original teaching and traditional text of *The Dhammapada* into our 21$^{st}$ century lifestyle, with a contemporary context. Without straying far from the Pali text it renders it in a fresh and modern idiom, with a universal appeal. An introduction provides a background to the life and times of the historical Buddha, and his teachings on the four noble truths and eight fold noble path.

Foreword by H.H. The Dalai Lama, with his seal of approval.

Karma Yonten Senge is a Dharma practitioner of the Karma Kagyu tradition of Tibetan Buddhism. He is an avid follower of Buddha Dharma, and currently lives in Australia.

1 905047 30 4
£9.99/$19.95

---

# Good As New

*A radical re-telling of the Christian Scriptures*
John Henson

This radical new translation conveys the early Christian scriptures in the idiom of today. It is "inclusive," following the principles which Jesus adopted in relation to his culture. It is women, gay and sinner friendly. It follows principles of cultural and contextual translation. It also returns to the selection of books that modern scholarship now agrees were held in most esteem by the early Church.

*A presentation of extraordinary power.*
**Rowan Williams**, Archbishop of Canterbury

*I can't rate this version of the Christian scriptures highly enough. It is amazingly fresh, imaginative, engaging and bold.*
**Adrian Thatcher**, Professor of Applied Theology, College of St Mark and St John, Plymouth

*I found this a literally shocking read. It made me think, it made me laugh, it made me cry, it made me angry and it made me joyful. It made me feel like an early Christian hearing these texts for the first time.*
**Elizabeth Stuart**, Professor of Christian Theology, King Alfred's College, Winchester

*It spoke to me with a powerful relevancy that challenged me to re-think all the things that I have been taught.*
**Tony Campolo**, Professor Emeritus of Sociology, Eastern University

*With an extraordinary vigour and immediacy,* Good As New *constantly challenges, surprises and delights you. Over and over again you feel like you're reading about Jesus for the first time.* Ship of Fools *John Henson,* a retired evangelical Baptist minister, has co-ordinated this translation over the last 12 years on behalf of *ONE for Christian Exploration*, a network of radical Christians and over twenty organisations in the UK

1-903816-74-2
£19.99 $29.95 hb
1-90504711-8
£11.99 $19.95 pb

---

# Is There An Afterlife?

*David Fontana*

The question whether or not we survive physical death has occupied the minds of men and women since the dawn of recorded history. The spiritual traditions of both West and East have taught that death is not the end, but modern science generally dismisses such teachings.

The fruit of a lifetime's research and experience by a world expert in the field, *Is There An Afterlife?* presents the most complete survey to date of the evidence, both historical and contemporary, for survival of physical death. It looks at the question of what survives-personality, memory, emotions and body image-in particular exploring the question of consciousness as primary to and not dependent on matter in the light of recent brain research and quantum physics. It discusses the possible nature of the afterlife, the common threads in Western and Eastern traditions, the common features of "many levels," group souls and reincarnation.

As well a providing the broadest overview of the question, giving due weight to the claims both of science and religion, *Is There An Afterlife?* brings it into personal perspective. It asks how we should live in this life as if death is not the end, and suggests how we should change our behaviour accordingly.

*David Fontana* is a Fellow of the British Psychological Society (BPS), Founder Chair of the BPS Transpersonal Psychology Section, Past President and current Vice President of the Society for Psychical Research, and Chair of the SPR Survival Research Committee. He is Distinguished Visiting Fellow at Cardiff University, and Professor of Transpersonal Psychology at Liverpool John Moores University. His many books on spiritual themes have been translated into 25 languages.

1 903816 90 4
£11.99/$16.95

---

# The Ocean of Wisdom

*Alan Jacobs*

*The most comprehensive anthology of spiritual wisdom available*

The first major anthology of this size and scope since 1935, *The Ocean of Wisdom* collects over five thousand pearls in poetry and prose, from the earliest of recorded history to modern times. Divided into 54 sections, ranging from Action to Zen, it draws on all faiths and traditions, from Zoroaster to existentialism. It covers the different ages of man, the stages of life, and is an ideal reference work and long term companion, a source of inspiration for the journey of life.

Frequently adopting a light touch it also makes a distinction between the Higher Wisdom, which consists of pointers leading to the understanding of philosophical and metaphysical truth, and practical wisdom, which consists of intelligent skills applicable to all fields of ordinary everyday life. So Germaine Greer and Hilary Rodham Clinton have their place alongside Aristotle and Sartre.

The carefully chosen quotations make this book the perfect bedside dipper, and will refresh the spirit of all who are willing to bathe in the ocean of the world's wisdom.

Few individuals have as wide an acquaintance with the world's traditions and scriptures as *Alan Jacobs*. He is Chairperson of the Ramana Maharshi Foundation (UK), editor of *Poetry of the Spirit*, and has translated *The Bhagavad Gita* (O Books), *The Principal Upanishads* (O Books) and *The Wisdom of Marcus Aurelius* (O Books).

1 905047 07 X
£19.95/$29.95

---

# The 7 Aha!s of Highly Enlightened Souls

Mike George

With thousands of insights now flooding the market place of spiritual development, how do we begin to decide where to start our spiritual journey? What are the right methods? This book strips away the illusions that surround the modern malaise we call stress. In 7 insights, it reminds us of the essence of all the different paths of spiritual wisdom. It succinctly describes what we need to realize in order to create authentic happiness and live with greater contentment. It finishes with the 7 AHA!S, the "eureka moments", the practice of any one of which will profoundly change your life in the most positive way.

Mike George is a spiritual teacher, motivational speaker, retreat leader and management development facilitator. He brings together the three key strands of his millennium-spiritual and emotional intelligence, leadership development, and continuous learning. His previous books include *Discover Inner Peace, Learn to Relax* and *In The Light of Meditation*.

1 903816 31 9
£5.99 $11.95

P. 133 'In learning to listen to...etc?